The Shearer Method
Classic Guitar Foundations

By Aaron Shearer, Thomas Kikta and Dr. Alan Hirsh

Editing: **Aaron Shearer, Alan Hirsh, Thomas Kikta**

All Compositions and Arrangements: **Alan Hirsh**

Layout Artist and Cover Design: **James Manly**

Cover Photograph: **Dave Garson**

Graphics Illustrator: **Sean O'Shea**

Camera Operators: **Alec Bosler and Justin Stag**

Audio Engineer: **Thomas Kikta**

Video Editor: **Thomas Kikta**

DVD Mastering: **Jamey Stewart - Mega Media Factory**

Audio Performances: **Thomas Kikta Classic Guitar**
Alyssa Ostrzyzek Flute

Guitar by: **John Martin Oribe - José Oribe & Co.**

Manuscript Assistant: **Andrew Motton**

Opening and Closing Voice Over: **Jeff Bergman**

Video and Audio Recorded at: **Brookside Studios, Pittsburgh, PA; Duquesne University Aaron Shearer Memorial Classic Guitar Studio; The Dr. Thomas D. Pappert Center for Performance and Innovation**

DVD Manufacturing: **Jesse Naus - Red Caiman Media Studios**

Special Thanks to Dr. Edward Kocher Dean of the Mary Pappert School of Music, Duquesne University, Aaron Stang and Lorraine Shearer.

Dedicated to the memory of Aaron Shearer, Lorraine Shearer, Thomas J. Kikta, M. Agnes Kikta and Leslie Weidner.

Aaron Shearer was one of the most widely recognized and respected classic guitar teachers in America. When Shearer started the Classic Guitar Department at American University it became the first classic guitar program in an American institution of higher learning. Subsequently, he was director of the guitar programs at Catholic University of America, Peabody Conservatory of Music, and the North Carolina School of the Arts. Towards the end of his life he was adjunct professor of Classic Guitar at Duquesne University. Mr. Shearer lectured throughout the United States and Canada, and received numerous citations for his contributions to guitar pedagogy. Shearer also became the first classic guitar teacher to be cited for exceptional leadership and merit by the American String Teachers Association and in 1992 received an Honorary Doctorate from Duquesne University.

During his lifetime he published numerous books and articles, including a six-book method entitled *Classic Guitar Technique* which included two volumes with three supplements and a guitar note speller. This benchmark method was originally published in 1959 and is now updated with CD in its 3rd edition by Alfred Publications. In 1992, Mr. Shearer published a three-part book entitled *Learning the Classic Guitar*. Shortly after, he began to experiment with alternative ways of supporting the guitar while still maintaining muscular alignment and full access to the instrument. His creation of the *Shearer Strap* has given guitarists freedom from the constraints of the footstool. In the early part of 2008, prior to his passing, He finished his magnum opus *The Shearer Method*, a comprehensive treatise that covers his entire approach to teaching and learning the classic guitar.

Aaron Shearer's body of work was revolutionary and his unwavering commitment to excellence earned him the moniker, "The Wall," by some of his students. The guitar world has referred to him, as "The Father of the American Classic Guitar". The Guitar Foundation of America has called him "the most prominent pedagogue of the twentieth century". Aaron Shearer's wisdom and insight are sorely missed, but his work and legacy will live on through the Aaron Shearer Foundation and all the lives he has touched.

Thomas Kikta as a musician, producer, professor and author is a versatile artist who has been the director of Classic Guitar and Recording Arts and Sciences at Duquesne University in Pittsburgh, PA. for over twenty five years.

A native of Pittsburgh, he studied Classic Guitar performance with Aaron Shearer at both the Peabody Conservatory and at the North Carolina School of the Arts. He has performed around the country and for such dignitaries as Maya Angelou and Toni Morrison and has worked with such artists as Ricardo Cobo, and Manuel Barrueco. After working closely with Aaron Shearer for over 28 years he with Mr. Shearer co-authored the 3rd edition of the best-selling and benchmark work *Classic Guitar Technique Vol 1* published by Alfred Publications, which was nominated for "Best Instructional Book or Video for 2009" by Music and Sound Retailer. He was invited to write *The Complete Idiots Guide to Classical Guitar Favorites* which was published by Alfred Publications in 2010. This work provides supplementary lessons to 30 favorite selections for a student working with a method book.

As a co-founder and Board Chairman of the Guitar Society of Fine Arts, Pittsburgh audiences have enjoyed a decade of world-class guitar music as well as free music lessons for underprivileged children. Thomas Kikta along with members of the Shearer family have founded the Aaron Shearer Foundation, an organization dedicated to preserving and propagating the teachings and legacy of this revolutionary guitar pedagogue.

Dr. Alan Hirsh received his Bachelor's in Composition from the University of Arizona and both his Masters and Doctorate from the Peabody Conservatory of the Johns Hopkins University in Baltimore, MD. Alan Hirsh teaches guitar and is the Fine Arts Department Chair at Bishop McGuinness High School in Kernersville, North Carolina. He also teaches adjunct at Wake Forest University in Winston-Salem, North Carolina and is the founder and director of the Piedmont Guitar Orchestra, since 1996. He actively directs clinics and festival guitar orchestra's around the country and serves on the executive board of the Aaron Shearer Foundation as well as the Piedmont Classic Guitar Society. Hirsh has composed and arranged extensively for orchestra, band, chorus, guitar and guitar ensemble with works performed around the world. In 1984, he collaborated with Aaron Shearer, composing music for the three-volume method, *Learning the Classic Guitar*. Hirsh's other original published works include *Twenty Etudes in fixed Positions*, *New Music for Classic Guitar*, a four-book collection of guitar ensemble music, as well as an extensive catalogue of guitar ensemble music online.

Table of Contents

Forward

I had the privilege of working with Aaron Shearer for over 28 years. I started in 1980, as a student at The Peabody Conservatory of Music at The Johns Hopkins University. When Aaron decided to continue his work at the North Carolina School of the Arts, I was one of the lucky eight chosen to follow him to Winston-Salem. In 1987, I received the Directorship of Classic Guitar at Duquesne University and he would often come to Pittsburgh to teach lessons and Performance Development Class. Ultimately, Aaron joined me at Duquesne in 1996 as an adjunct faculty member and we developed a close friendship-writing, teaching and developing guitar curriculum.

He first started talking about writing *The Shearer Method* around 1998. He wanted an opportunity to define his methodology and share his thoughts and insights from over 70 years of playing and teaching the classic guitar. As we discussed the various attributes of such a work it became obvious that technology would play a very important part in telling this story. Together we purchased VHS-C cameras and through crude internet video connections between Pennsylvania and North Carolina, we worked to develop the format and concepts that effectively presented his method. Each chapter was written with the knowledge that his writing would be supported by my video presentations.

In the beginning of 2008, he came to me with a finished manuscript and said "here it is…it's really good…shoot the videos, write the forward and get this thing published because I won't be here to see it." It was all so surreal, it reminded me too much of the last scene from the movie *Finding Forrester* with William Forrester telling Jamal Wallace to write the forward to his last novel and get it published because he was dying. Aaron's words were prophetic because by April of 2008 he was gone; passing away quietly with friends and family around him. In addition to the extreme sadness that I felt in losing my teacher and friend, what hit me was the profound responsibility that was put upon my shoulders to see that a work of such importance be finished.

Working in high definition video, we started shooting the scripts that would become 63 presentations that highlight Aaron's work. We felt that this material deserved custom musical selections and etudes so Alan Hirsh began writing over 70 wonderful selections that are simple for the student but so musically beautiful. Aaron's wife, Lorraine Shearer, would call to find out how things were progressing, encouraging us and providing all kinds of support that was instrumental to the success of this project of which I am so very grateful. Together we recorded, shot, composed and revised to make the work that you now hold in your hands.

The Shearer Method Classic Guitar Foundations is the first in a series of works that define Aaron Shearer's approach to study—**how** to play the guitar. This work stands by itself in starting the student to read and play while promoting a curriculum flow that supports positive habits for efficient study. The student will progress to the point where truly interesting and beautiful music will be created and leave with a foundational technique that will serve them well as they experience more challenging subjects; setting the stage for Aaron's more complex writings.

It has been an honor to work on this project, to be a part of the talented team that made this a reality and to be a member of the network that carries on Aaron Shearer's legacy.

He has truly given us a gift that we all benefit from…and now you will too.

Enjoy

Thomas Kikta

The Shearer Method
Classic Guitar Foundations

Preface
DEVELOPING THE ABILITY TO PERFORM WELL WITH SECURITY AND CONFIDENCE

During the years since writing my *Classic Guitar Technique* and *Learning the Classic Guitar* books my approach to guitar study has undergone a number of significant improvements. Although many of the terms and ideas remain the same, some differ in application, others have been replaced, and some important new ones have been added. The current approach (which includes an explanatory DVD with Video and Audio Tracks) presents a shift in emphasis, both from my previous books, and from other guitar methods I have seen.

This shift in emphasis reflects my conviction about the ultimate goal of guitar study: developing the ability to perform well with security and confidence. Performance, for our purposes, means playing for an attentive audience—be it in a concert hall or one's own home. Although the phrase 'perform well' may seem self-explanatory, in this text it conveys the special meaning of consistently fulfilling the artistic expectations of both the performer and the listener.

The expectations of the listener depend on a number of considerations, but audiences generally seek an expressive performance which demands reasonable accuracy, presented with spirit, ease, and conviction. The performer's expectations are also quite complex, but there is one in particular that is often overlooked: the performer's need to enjoy performing. To do this, one must not only engage with the music, but also have confidence that one will perform well every time. This confidence comes from a deep sense of security—a complete trust in one's ability to achieve a high standard of playing in each performance.

The main impediment to this kind of performing can often be attributed to "performance anxiety" or "stage fright." When severe, this condition can be incapacitating—but even when mild it is an unpleasant hindrance. The causes of performance anxiety may seem elusive, but the problem is so pervasive that it is frequently the topic of books and articles. Wide-spread performance anxiety results from fear of failure and the resulting humiliation. Even so, it strongly appears that nearly all students dedicated enough to learn to play an instrument have a natural desire to share music with others, and to earn admiration for their effort.

Unfortunately, many talented students and even advanced professionals are denied such positive experiences because of the crippling effects of performance anxiety. The approach outlined in this method is the product of an effort to minimize performance anxiety by developing positive performance habits from the very earliest stages of training. The result is effective not only because of the quality or accuracy of the information, but also because of the step-by-step presentation. Information will be introduced only when it is needed and has immediate application. The outcome is a gradual process of learning that leads most quickly to habits of security and confidence, and positive feelings of progress—both essential parts of enjoying guitar study. The emphasis on forming these habits (which are the product of the student's thought process) have prompted a fuller focus on the mental aspects of learning to play the guitar—on the dominant role of the mind. This role of the mind is the primary focus of the Introduction and will remain a thread of continuity throughout the entire Method.

USING THE MULTIMEDIA DISC

This book comes with a single disc that contains all of the multimedia presentations, both *video* and *audio*. The videos play in a standard DVD player or computer but the audio (TNT2 encoded) *will only* work in your computer. The book serves as the foundation for the method. However, subjects that require clarification beyond the text are demonstrated in the accompanying videos which visually help you to form better understanding. As you work through this book, refer to videos whenever you see the 📀 symbol. The concepts involved in learning the classic guitar can often be complex—feel free to review both the text and videos frequently.

In addition, the audio portion of the disc contains all of the duets, and a few helpful selections from the solo pieces. Refer to these whenever you see the audio symbol 🔊. The audio plays on any computer using the TNT2 (*Tone and Tempo*) software that comes with the disc. This allows you to:

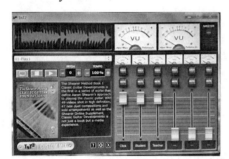

- speed up or slow down tempo.
- control the volume for each track.
- *solo* the student's or teacher's part.
- turn the metronome on or off.
- loop sections to repeatedly rehearse them.

(See the multimedia disc instructions opposite the media disc pouch.)

ABOUT THE SHEARER ONLINE SUPPLEMENT

The *Shearer Online Supplement* found at **www.aaronshearerfoundation.org** contains articles that, while providing essential information for learning to play the guitar well, are of a length or complexity that's more suitable outside the present text. Further, the *Supplement* also contains articles that, along with being interesting, are meant to provide the enterprising student a factual, well-rounded view of the often confusing world of guitar instruction. Thus the text and the *Supplement* are interdependent. The text becomes more meaningful through applying information found in the *Supplement* and the *Supplement* makes orderly sense only when used in conjunction with the text; this relationship is noted in using the www symbol placed in the outer margins throughout the text. When you see this be sure to visit the corresponding article at www.aaronshearerfoundation.org. In addition to the *Shearer Online Supplement,* you will find other resources for students, teachers and performers interested in learning more about Aaron Shearer's work.

THE TWO KINDS OF GUITARS

The guitar family can be divided into two distinct branches: those with nylon strings, which are usually sounded with the fingers of the right hand, and those with steel strings (with which we will include electric guitars), which are usually sounded with a plectrum or pick.

The nylon-string guitar produces sound through a resonating body. The steel-string guitar produces sound through a body and/or electronic amplification. The steel-string guitar is mainly used in playing popular and folk styles of music, and although the nylon-string guitar can be used to play all kinds of music, it is generally used in playing classical music.

"CLASSIC" OR "CLASSICAL" GUITAR?

The nylon-string guitar is commonly known by two related names: the classic guitar and the classical guitar. Since both names adequately distinguish this guitar from its steel-stringed relative, I readily accept either. Thus, using one term or the other has never been a major issue with me. Though like many other guitarists, I've chosen one term in preference to the other. The following are my reasons.

"Classical guitar" may have arisen because much of the guitar's early development and repertoire dates from the Classical period of music (1750-1830). Granted, the guitar does have important roots in the Classical Period. The overall design and construction of the modern guitar, however, were developed by Antonio Torres (1817-1892). His remarkable innovations date from around 1850—well after the Classical period ended. Further, "classical" can be misleading, suggesting that this type of guitar is suited only for classical music.

To me, "classic guitar" seems more appropriate. According to *Webster's Dictionary,* classic means "of recognized value: serving as a standard of excellence; traditional, enduring." Also, the term "classic" is somewhat more distinctive than "classical." There are many pieces of music that date from the Classical period which have never become classics. Something becomes classic through the test of time. Thus, it's accurate to say that, among the various types of guitar, ours is the "classic" guitar.

EXAMINING THE PARTS OF THE CLASSIC GUITAR

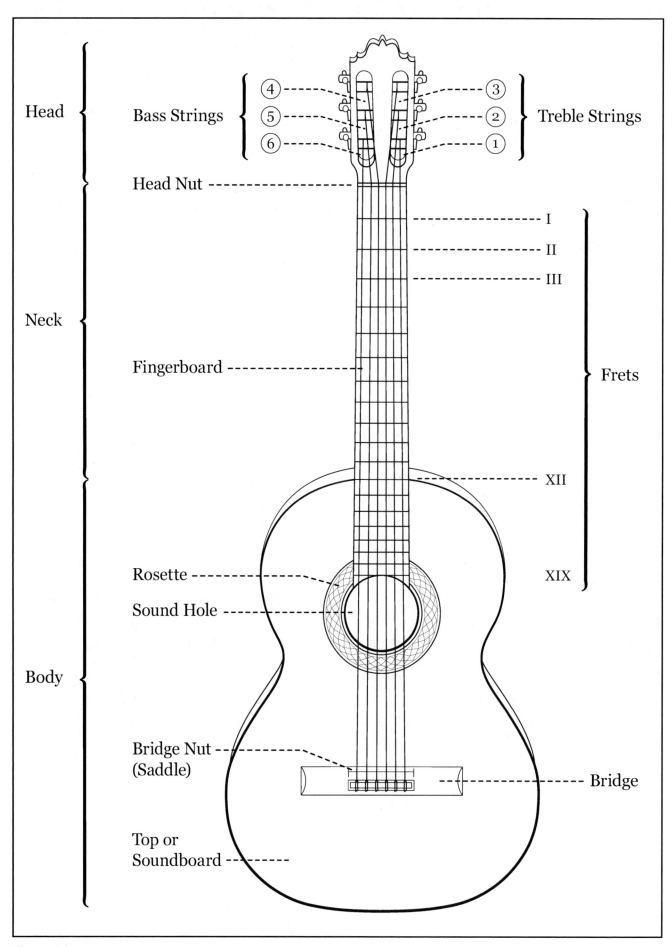

Figure 1A

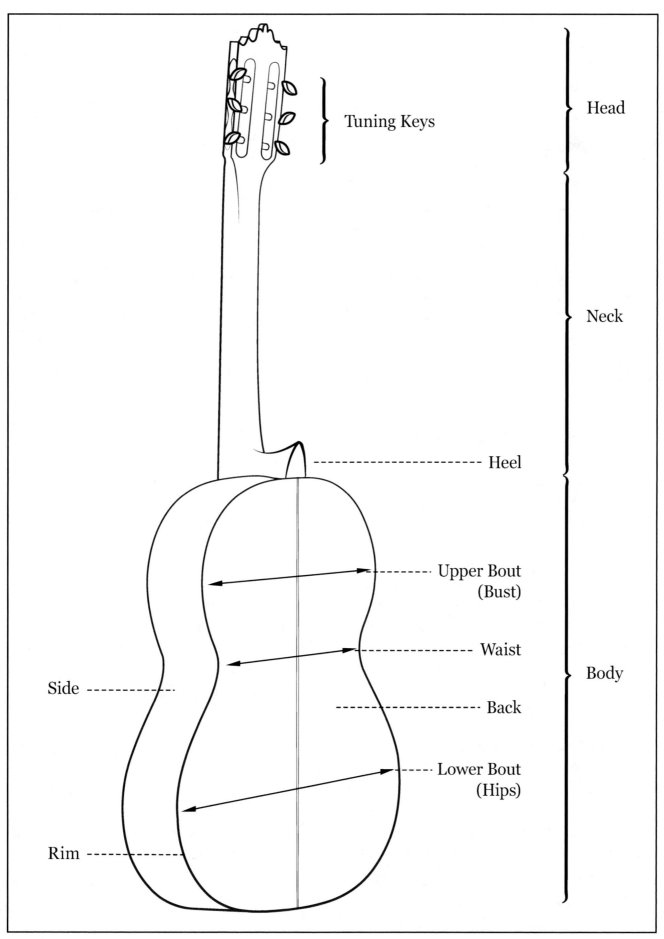

Tuning Keys

Head

Neck

Heel

Upper Bout
(Bust)

Waist

Side

Back

Body

Lower Bout
(Hips)

Rim

Figure 1B

ATTACHING THE STRINGS

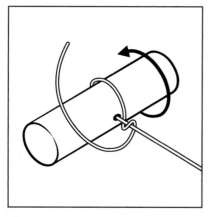

Figure 2A

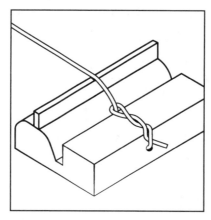

Figure 2B

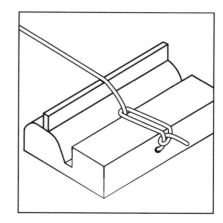

Figure 2C

Notice how in Fig. 2A a string is attached to the roller pin on the tuning keys. Common ways of attaching the other end of the string to the bridge are illustrated in Figs. 2B and 2C. Be sure when tying a string to the bridge that the last turn of the string is secured behind the back edge of the bridge. Tied in this manner, the string will be less likely to slip when it is brought up to pitch.

SELECTING THE RIGHT SIZE GUITAR

The size of your guitar can strongly influence your progress in learning to play. If you are of small stature, attempting to learn on a full-size guitar would be awkward and extremely difficult if not impossible. Some teachers are aware of this problem and wisely recommend guitars of a suitable size for their students; regrettably, many teachers do not give this issue proper attention. Guitar teachers would do well to emulate the long-standing tradition of teachers of the violin and cello who long ago demanded that makers of those instruments provide a variety of sizes. One well-known catalogue lists eight sizes of violins and six sizes of cellos. In addition to the full-size guitar, reasonably priced *quarter-size, half- size,* and *three quarter- size* nylon-string guitars have become available at music stores and studios where the classic guitar is taught. Although the final decision about the most suitable size guitar should be made by an experienced teacher, the following guide may be helpful in selecting the proper guitar for a student.

Assuming that the student has a classic guitar, the main concern is with the guitar's length relative to the height of the student when he or she is standing. This is determined with the lower end of the guitar resting on the floor with its head pointed upward while the guitar is held close to the student's side. Try to choose a guitar whose head extends preferably to the lower ribcage or hip area. Keep in mind that these recommendations are approximate and that it's better to select a guitar that is somewhat smaller than one that is too large.

SOME NECESSARY ACCESSORIES

In addition to the guitar, you will need the following accessories:

Positioning appliance to maintain good playing posture (The Classic Guitar Strap kit is highly recommended—See *Positioning the Guitar,* p.viii).

Electronic guitar tuner to ensure that your guitar will always sound properly tuned.

Music stand to ensure proper body positioning when practicing.

DVD player and computer.

Metronome to help you to feel and understand rhythms.

CHOOSING A TEACHER

It is difficult to overstate the importance of choosing the right teacher; your teacher will influence nearly every aspect of your musical experience, from how well you play to how much you enjoy learning the guitar. Beginners usually lack the knowledge to accurately evaluate a teacher. It is with this in mind that the following simple guidelines have been provided to assist this important decision.

1) **Don't choose a teacher solely on the merits of his or her apparent playing ability.** The skills of teaching and playing are quite different; not all great players are great teachers, and not all great teachers are great players.

2) **If you decide to use this method, you should find a teacher who advocates this approach to learning the guitar.** While I have tried to be as clear as possible in the presentation of material in this book, every student is unique. You will progress much more quickly with a teacher familiar with the present material who can tailor it to your specific needs.

3) **Don't be reluctant to ask questions based on what you've learned from reading this book.** It is important to take an active role in your musical education; by asking questions you can be sure that your teacher will be able to communicate effectively with you.

ABOUT TUNING THE GUITAR

The tuning method practiced by most professionals is tuning by ear. This tuning method requires the ability to relate and compare very slight differences in pitch, and the ability to produce very consistent sounds on the instrument. In the past, this situation posed serious problems for the developing guitarist and required a great deal of patience from relatives and other who were obliged to listen. Luckily the development of the electronic guitar tuner has provided a means to easily and accurately tune the instrument without requiring an advanced sense of pitch on the part of the guitarist. Electronic tuners are widely available and have become reasonably inexpensive. By using a tuner during your early development you will acquire the habit of hearing the guitar "in tune" in preparation for learning to tune by ear. A person at your local music store can instruct you on how to use one.

ABOUT THE PLAYING CONDITION OF YOUR GUITAR

The playing condition of your guitar is extremely important; if the strings are set too high over the fingerboard, they will be difficult to press firmly against the frets making the guitar unsuitable for learning to play. If the strings are set too low, when played they will vibrate against the frets and produce unclear buzzing sounds. A more detailed explanation of this topic can be found at www.aaronshearerfoundation.org in the *Shearer Method Online Supplement* , but the guitar should be thoroughly examined by a guitar maker or someone qualified to apply the information in that article.

HOLDING AND POSITIONING THE GUITAR

The primary issue of technical development that students need to consider in approaching the classic guitar is the powerful influence that the manner of holding the instrument has on all aspects of learning to play. We will begin our discussion of holding and positioning the guitar by clarifying our aim: We should try to learn the guitar with the greatest possible sense of ease. In general, we can associate comfort with ease and discomfort with difficulty. Thus "most comfortable" defines the best position for training the hands—the position which offers the most progress for the amount of time and effort involved in study and practice.

To discuss training the hands, it's essential to realize that the hands unavoidably reflect the state of the muscles of the torso that support the arms and hands. If the back and shoulders are comfortably balanced and aligned, the arms and hands more readily assume a state of dynamic relaxation most conducive to training. Feelings of comfort and discomfort powerfully dictate the response of muscles to training: when one is comfortable, the muscles are trained more easily; when one is uncomfortable, training the muscles is more difficult. The body mechanism which signals a misuse of muscles does not make mistakes; repeated feelings of strain and discomfort are clear indications that muscles are being misused.

While the physical aspects of positioning are extremely important, a further highly negative consequence of the discomfort of negative positioning should be kept in mind: *Not only does such misuse of muscles impede the efficient development of technique, but it's an unavoidable distraction that also hinders development of the well-focused concentration essential in learning to play the guitar well.*

Use of the footstool, begun in the early 1800's and still widely used today, does not provide the means for positioning the guitar in an acceptably comfortable playing position because it forces misalignment of the muscles in the back. By the mid 1800's there was concrete evidence that guitarists had begun questioning use of the traditional footstool.

The widespread use of the footstool presents a difficult situation that, through tradition, has undoubtedly existed ever since the guitar began to be recognized as worthy of serious study. Many years ago, I became aware of the problems inherent in positioning with a footstool and made several attempts to solve them. Then, sometime during 2001, I experienced a conceptual breakthrough which eventually resulted in the present design of what has become known as *The Shearer Classic Guitar Strap*. My experience has shown that proper use of this device as explained in the *Guitar Positioning Handbook* included in the Strap Kit, and also in the DVD, solves the important problems outlined above. Students should carefully read the comprehensive article titled *A Brief History of Positioning the Guitar* appearing in *The Supplement*, which also covers the strap's development.

Use of a Footrest

The general design of the guitar and how it must be played has obviously posed serious physical problems for players ever since the instrument was invented—problems which have never been satisfactorily solved. Presumably to hold the guitar more securely and to provide freer access to the fingerboard, sometime during the late 1800's guitarists began placing the guitar on the left thigh elevated through use of a footrest. Further, in quest of a more effective functioning of the left hand, it was found necessary, in using a footrest, to twist the spine through turning and leaning to the left thus causing severe tension (and often pain) throughout the back and shoulders. Although the spread of such counterproductive tension to both hands is unavoidable, this is, after over a century, still the most widely employed method of positioning the guitar.

The Adjustable Footrest is Introduced

With the thought that it would be advantageous for guitarists of various sizes and builds to be able to adjust the height of the footstool, I began in the early 1950's to experiment with such a device. When my Classic Guitar Technique Book was first published by G. Ricordi in 1959, my new "footrest," adjustable up to nine inches in height, was advertised on the inside of the back cover at $4.95.[1] Although the adjustable feature appeared to be an improvement, I soon saw that even more elevation of the thigh was needed and began providing my students with styrofoam pads shaped to fit the contour of the thigh on one surface and the guitar on the opposite surface used along with the footrest. Some of my well-known former students still use such a pad. Guitarists in general who do not use a pad often resort to an extremely high footrest which elevates the left thigh to an acute uncomfortable angle with the sharply bent left knee pointed toward the ceiling. The effect of this unnatural posture on the already contorted spine and muscles of the back does not, of course, solve the problem of holding the guitar far enough to the right to meet the left hand requirements posed by Aguado. However, by rotating and leaning the torso to the left (which often results in serious back fatigue and even pain) a somewhat more effective left hand approach to the fingerboard can be achieved than with a lower footrest.

The A-Frame Is Invented

About a decade ago, some 140 years after Sor and Aguado, the first true innovation for positioning the guitar became available. The A-Frame, which I assume most guitarists have seen or at least heard about, was invented jointly by Robert Driggers, a design engineer, and David Stevenson, the guitar instructor at the University of North Carolina, Asheville. Its main advantage is that alone, or perhaps when used along with a footrest, it permits elevating the guitar with less discomfort. However, for reasons that will soon be apparent, the A-Frame does not solve other significant problems in positioning the guitar.

---

[1] Whether my Port-A-Just Footstand was the first adjustable footrest to be marketed and whether I was the first to advocate use of a thigh pad, are not major concerns to me. If there were other such devices being used, and I rather assume there might have been, I simply did not learn about them until several years later. As is well known, when my footrest became unavailable, others of similar design replaced it and are widely used today.

Determining the Optimal Playing Position

Sometime during the early part of the year 2000, it occurred to me that, at least to my knowledge, the optimal playing position had never been clearly defined. Thus I decided to try an experiment that, if successful, would provide an answer to this vexing question. Taking my cue from Aguado, the experiment would center on the left hand while providing for a viable right hand position. This thought led to my holding the guitar in an approximate playing position with my right hand, while standing, and then shifting the instrument alternately up and down, to the right and the left, and angling the neck higher and lower while executing a six string bar at the first fret as well as other normally challenging left hand formations. Only a few minutes of testing clearly revealed that the strongest, most comfortable functioning of the left hand fingers requires that the wrist be relatively straight which results from the guitar being placed substantially higher and farther to the right than is customary.

By continuing to hold the guitar (with the right hand) in this same position when seated, the two main reasons why the A-Frame is not an adequate solution to positioning the guitar became apparent: As it is currently designed and used, this device does not permit elevating the guitar high enough nor placing it far enough to the right to achieve optimal comfort of the left wrist and hand. This position called for a radical change in the approach to positioning the guitar; that change would prove to be a new application of a device that has been widely used for many years on almost all types of guitars except the classic guitar—the shoulder strap.

Advantages of Using the Shearer Classic Guitar Strap

I had considered use of a strap in the past, but because my objectives were not clearly defined I had dismissed it as impractical for holding the classic guitar—as many other guitarists had probably done. That it is now becoming recognized as practical, is due primarily to the following reasons:

- The advantages of holding the guitar higher and farther to the right than is traditional have been clarified. This has resulted in a new approach to placing and attaching the strap to the classic guitar. (To distinguish this from shoulder straps used on other kinds of guitars, in this writing, it is hereafter referred to as my Classic Guitar Strap.)
- By providing an overall well-balanced seating posture with the legs kept closer together and both feet flat on the floor, an entirely unprecedented level of comfort in playing the classic guitar is achieved.
- It provides optimal mechanical functioning of the hands further contributing to comfort and ease.
- It provides mobility. The guitarist can move expressively when performing seated, and can maintain a very similar playing position for the hands while standing. (See the DVD, also see the Strap Handbook and negative effect of discomfort on developing concentration and visualization included with the strap)

Introducing the Classic Guitar Strap to Experienced Guitarists

When introducing the classic shoulder-strap to a guitarist who has become accustomed to playing in a position resulting in varying degrees of discomfort, it is strongly recommended that the procedure of self-discovery previously described above under the heading, Determining the Optimal Playing Position be carried out. Once the most comfortable and effective position is determined, the strap can often seem like a godsend. Depending on the natural mental and physical flexibility of the individual, even some guitarists who have been playing many years, almost immediately perceive the advantages of the strap. Others must take time to experiment and consider the ramifications of making the change. We know that deeply ingrained habits tend to resist changes involving various mental adjustments and muscular regrouping. Acquiring new habits will demand some time and patient practice before the full benefits from using the strap can be realized. But when such adjustments are perceived as making playing far easier and better, they can occur quite rapidly (see also the article "A Brief History of Positioning the Guitar" found in the Supplement at www.aaronshearerfoundation.org)

A Final Thought on Seating Position

It needs to be mentioned that seating position is a very personal subject; what might work well for one individual could feel uncomfortable for another. With continued experimentation, the resulting evolution of your seating position is inevitable. Be sensitive to any discomfort or tension that might develop but realize any new position will feel unusual until habits are formed. Just be sure that these are habits that follow the concepts supported in this method. It can be said that the refinement of seating position is directly proportionate to the difficulty of the music being played. In the beginning simple pieces may not demand a lot of your seating position but as selections become more complex, it will be essential for you to have a seating position that promotes free access to the instrument.

CONCERNING THE RIGHT-HAND NAILS: FUNDAMENTAL NAIL SHAPE

The beautiful tone heard on recordings and in recitals is achieved by using the nails. However, most teachers recommend that young students, and even some more mature students, not attempt to use nails during the early stages of training. It is important to be aware, however, that initially the use of nails feels quite different, but that the tone is far more satisfying than when nails are not used. The teacher should tell the student when it is appropriate to begin using nails, but considering that habits of finger movement form rapidly and that eventually the student will use nails, it makes sense to start using them as soon as they can be grown and kept at an adequate length.

ON THE IMPORTANCE OF A TEACHER

As previously indicated, the most rewarding way to use this book and the DVD is with the direction of a good teacher. If you are a beginner—considering that the term "beginner" can refer to a broad range of students from the very young to an older adult—attempting to begin study of the guitar without a proficient teacher is impractical. If you already play the guitar and want to improve, a competent teacher would unquestionably make improvement easier and faster. In any case, whether you are a beginner or already play, or whether you are fortunate enough to have the guidance of a capable teacher, most of the time you spend in study and practice must be in solitude. This fact comes to light by considering the reality of studying with a teacher: The usual duration of a weekly lesson for a mature student is one hour and much less for younger students. During that time, the teacher must not only listen to you play and provide directions for your improvement, but must also explain and assign material for study during the following week. It's in applying your teacher's directions along with using those found in the book and the DVD throughout the week that you must be your own teacher.

Then there is the extremely important matter of *constant review* of material already studied. Many aspects of playing the guitar depend on habits acquired through repeated study and careful practice—through review. Consistent review should be regarded as crucial in obtaining the most benefit from the use of this Method.

Introduction
Essential Concepts for Efficient Guitar Study

The following pages present concepts which form the foundation of this approach to learning the guitar. Habitual application of these concepts will make learning to play easier and will help the student eliminate performance anxiety. Teachers should refer to these concepts frequently and share them in a meaningful way with each student.

Concerning the Role of the Mind in Learning the Guitar

During my youth, I became aware that all voluntary movements, such as those involving the hands, are directed by the mind. Many years would pass, however, before I began to relate this insight in any specific way to learning the guitar. Decades later, after I became more deeply involved in the process of learning to play the guitar, another level of understanding began to emerge. Gradually, I became aware that the mind has the dominant role in playing and even in learning to play the guitar. This led to the thought that in any learning situation the mind can function only according to the information it receives, which prompted a further conclusion: to learn the guitar efficiently, all students must try to provide the mind with accurate and relevant information. It is with this thought that we proceed to explore how to set such a process in motion.

OUR FOUR NATURAL ABILITIES

Students need to realize that there are four natural abilities—basic mental tools that we all possess for learning to play and perform music on the guitar: *visualizing, concentrating, acquiring habits, and forming aims.* Natural abilities differ from learned abilities because they occur automatically. Since they are inborn, we cannot claim credit for having our natural abilities, but using and positively developing them is the responsibility of teachers and ultimately each individual student. This is the pathway to learning that everyone must follow—from the casual hobbyist to the gifted, highly intuitive prodigy. The main difference between the two is in the pace at which they can perceive and apply these concepts, and in their final level of achievement. An effective approach to developing these natural abilities will result in the easiest and most rapid development of the student. An ineffective approach will require a great deal more effort—effort directed towards overcoming the approach, rather than towards overcoming any natural difficulty in playing the instrument.

The Ability to Acquire Habits

We all acquire and function largely by habit, which, as may seem obvious, presents serious consequences for daily living. We also know that there are good habits and bad habits. Students need to be keenly aware of the crucial role that habits play in learning the skills needed to perform well on the guitar, and that such skills require *positive habits of thought that produce positive habits of movement* acquired through accurate repetition. It's essential to keep in mind that the process of forming habits occurs automatically *from the beginning of study* and significantly impacts your efficiency in learning to perform well with confidence.

Repetitions that are based on valid information and are carried out with accuracy and security will build habits of playing with accuracy and security, and will provide the foundation for performing expressively with freedom and confidence. Repetitions based on faulty information and carried out with confusion and error will build habits of confusion, error, insecurity, and anxiety. *This is a natural law of habit formation that operates constantly and functions with varying consistency for everyone.* Further, your ability to perform effective repetitions depends on having *clear aims* and habits of *reliable concentration*—acquired as explained here and throughout the text. Your primary goal is to experience the satisfaction of playing well, both alone as a personal accomplishment and in sharing your music with others. *Therefore, it is essential for you to practice thoughtfully in order to acquire only those habits that you want to occur in performance.* Preparation for achieving this ideal requires a clear understanding and effective application of both Visualization and Concentration.

The Natural Abilities to Visualize and Concentrate

The terms *visualize* and *visualization* apply not only to the visual sense, but to all mental images; to everything our minds can conceive, from the most concrete and tangible to the most abstract and intangible—*to mental images of all aspects of positioning, moving and touching, and to the many facets of sound and expression.* Accurate visualization provides the foundation for efficiently developing all areas of playing the guitar—in developing technique as well as the ability to read and expressively interpret music.

Concentration is much more easily defined than visualization. It is our ability to focus the mind on something specific: a task, an idea—truthfully anything at all. The possibility of not being able to concentrate sufficiently in performance is widely recognized as perhaps the greatest single concern among all levels of performers. Developing concentration begins with understanding the interdependent relationship between visualization and concentration.

Clarifying the Relationship between Visualization and Concentration

Effective visualization cannot exist without concentration and vice versa. Concentration is intangible and not entirely subject to our direct control. We can control concentration only indirectly through visualization, which is tangible and readily subject to our control. Thus visualization is our means for developing concentration. Since visualization demands concentration, it follows that developing the ability to visualize implies developing the ability to concentrate clearly. Therefore, it is insufficient to tell hesitant students to "concentrate," because this focuses on the wrong thing: the problem is the student's lack of ability to visualize sufficiently. Concerns about insufficient concentration are powerfully influenced by habits of faulty visualization often formed during early development.

Students need to be aware that we unavoidably acquire either positive habits of reliable visualization and concentration resulting in security, confidence, and continuity in performance or we acquire negative habits of unreliable visualization and concentration resulting in confusion, error, and hesitation in performance—the true source of performance anxiety. Developing the ability to visualize clearly is most effective when carried out gradually as an integral part of overall training—the approach used in this Method.

The Natural Ability to Form Aims

The fourth natural ability is the ability to form aims. Aims are intentions to accomplish things; they provide the pathways to all learning *and so are part of our normal thought process.* In learning to play and in playing the guitar there are two kinds of aims: technical and musical. Technical aims refer to all aspects of body positioning and movement. Musical aims refer to decisions about what music to play and to performing notes in various rhythms, to all aspects of dynamics (loudness or softness), tone quality, and to all other considerations pertaining to playing with effective expression.

In the beginning of guitar study, the two types of aims (technical and musical) must be more or less separated. Later they become interdependent—almost unified. A technical aim is a visualized intention of *where, what, when, and how* to move, resulting in the inclusive term "Aim Directed Movement" (ADM). Musical aims develop from a progressive study of all aspects of music including rhythm, pitches, dynamics, and tone. This requires developing one's musical ear through much careful listening approached in a context of learning to play music through the use of counting and spoken syllables to clarify such aims. Although we all automatically form both kinds of aims, their accuracy depends on the clarity of our thoughts.

Developing the ability to efficiently form accurate aims requires an easily understood process. In starting technical development, we acquire information from hearing and seeing the guitar played and ideally from a well-written text, along with a capable teacher's explanation and demonstration; this process initiates visualized aims of positioning and movement. But for these aims to become truly meaningful requires thoughtful experimenting in practice and using the information thus acquired to discover personally how it can most effectively be applied. This provides the basis for clarifying visualized aims—for making valid decisions about what needs to be done and how that can best be accomplished. Information, acquired through further instruction, listening, observation and personal discovery, provides increasingly refined aims. This is the constantly evolving process of clarifying and applying aims in learning to play the guitar from the first steps of the beginner to the lofty accomplishments of the virtuoso.

Confirming Aims through Speech

A simple, yet highly effective, approach to confirming technical aims that all students can readily carry out is for each to give a *verbal explanation* of how he or she intends to proceed. Naturally the extent and clarity of the spoken explanation will vary considerably depending on the maturity, background, and talent of the individual student. The important issue initially is not how detailed and comprehensive the explanation is, but that the student, on his or her level of perception, is prompted to concentrate on and become active in the process of forming and retaining clear aims. The mental/physical act of verbally explaining one's aims for establishing an idea and carrying out a movement induces a far clearer and more tangible mental vision of the intended procedure than a silent mental image alone. Accordingly, while serving to confirm effective aims in establishing a movement, verbal explanation prior to moving often exposes unclear aims and even misconceptions. The act of speaking is so effective that it might well be regarded as the most direct and tangible link we possess between thought and action—between visualization, aims, and movement leading to the formation of good habits. The verbal clarification of musical aims must be further explained through application, additional demonstration and evaluation by the teacher.

TO THE TEACHER:

A Further Beneficial Application of Speech

The use of speech as a powerful learning tool is highly effective in areas other than simply clarifying aims. After briefly reviewing with the student the main points covered in the preceding section on the *Essential Concepts for Efficient Guitar Study,* it's extremely helpful to verify this understanding of those concepts by asking questions appropriate for the individual student to prompt a spoken response. As with "aims," the extent of the response will vary widely depending on the maturity, background, and talent of the student. In any case this procedure will effectively consolidate, on his or her level, the student's knowledge of this extremely important area of the learning process. All students should soon be able to demonstrate an understanding of the following:

- The role of the mind
- The role of habits
- The meaning and role of visualization and its relationship to concentration
- The role of aims and how they are clarified

Again, as with the spoken explanation of aims, the important issue is not how detailed and comprehensive the response is but that the student is prompted initially to focus upon and clarify each of the four subjects in question. A verbal exchange has been shown to have value far beyond its benefits directly in learning to play; it's also effective in releasing inhibitions, building confidence in expressing oneself verbally and musically, and establishing a rapport with the teacher.

SUMMARY

We have briefly considered the dominant role of the mind, as well as the important innate abilities to acquire habits, to visualize and concentrate, and to form aims. Since all four of these abilities function according to the dominant role of the mind principle, everyone unavoidably (and usually unknowingly) applies them in normal, everyday activities—but not on the refined level required for playing the guitar well. We focus attention on these abilities here because their most efficient development cannot be accomplished intuitively, but requires careful, well-directed effort. In the process of learning the guitar, habits of confusion and error are more easily acquired than habits of precise thought and movement. Our natural abilities to visualize, concentrate and form aims tend naturally to resist functioning with clarity and accuracy. But depending upon the individual student's level of talent and dedication, he or she will respond to well directed study and practice. There is an old saying that students sometimes find meaningful: "If you think education is a drag, try ignorance!" (Derek Bok, President of Harvard from 1971-91.) **Similarly, if you think learning to visualize effectively is hard, try performing with habits of confusion, error and anxiety!**

Beginning Technical Development

Seated in the Optimal Playing Position as described in the Preface p.x and DVD 2, proceed to the following hand checks to evaluate your seating position.

CHECKING THE LEFT HAND

With the guitar positioned as shown in the DVD, check left-hand access to the full range of the fingerboard by placing the 1ˢᵗ finger across all six strings at the first fret. Then move the hand so that you can place the 4ᵗʰ (little) finger at the highest fret, at the sound hole. When this positioning procedure is carried out properly, the left shoulder will not need to be lowered to avoid (or minimize) wrist strain in placing the 1ˢᵗ finger at the first fret, and the highest fret can be reached with minimal displacement of the hand and without strain.

CHECKING THE RIGHT HAND

The right hand should be able to reach all six strings by moving only from the elbow. Practice by swinging your arm up and down from the elbow, carrying your hand across all six strings as shown in the DVD.

BEGINNING RIGHT-HAND TRAINING

Names of the Right Hand Thumb and Fingers

Although learning to play the guitar begins with training the right thumb (*p*), you need also to learn the names of the fingers since they serve the important role of stabilizing the hand during this early stage of study.

The Right Hand (R.H.) thumb and fingers are generally identified by the italicized letters: *p*, *i*, *m*, *a*, *c*,[2] as shown in Fig. 3:

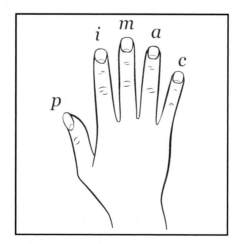

Figure 3

---

[2] These are the italicized first letters of the Spanish terms: *pulgar* (thumb), *indice* (index finger), *medio* (middle finger), *anular* (ring finger), and *chico* (little finger).

Names of the Right-Hand Thumb and Finger Joints

Effectively training the R.H. thumb and fingers begins by knowing the names of the joints:

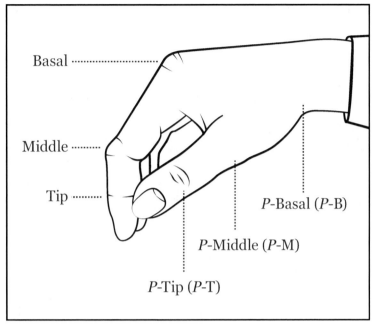

Figure 4

APPROACHING THE OPTIMAL HAND POSITION

The goal in the beginning is to establish solid foundations upon which all of your technique is built. For the right hand, this means finding the most effective position for creating optimal leverage at the wrist, finger and thumb joints. This position, shown in Fig. 4, is called the *Optimal Hand Position*. To learn how to find your optimal hand position, consider the following:

Flexion and Extension

Describing how to achieve optimal leverage at these joints requires use of the terms *flexion* and *extension:* Flexion at the wrist is "arching" toward the forearm; extension is the opposite of flexion. Flexion of a finger is movement toward the palm; flexion of the thumb is movement toward the side of the index finger.[3] As with the wrist, extension of a finger or the thumb is the opposite of flexion.

---

[3] This definition of thumb flexion and extension, while it is not scientifically accurate, is more readily understood and is therefore better suited for our purpose.

3

Midway Position and Midrange Movement of Joints

The *midway position* of finger joints is halfway between the comfortable limits of flexion and extension. Recognition of the midway position of finger joints is essential in achieving the optimal hand position. The *midrange movement* of finger joints falls approximately within the middle two quarters of the area between the comfortable limits of flexion and extension.

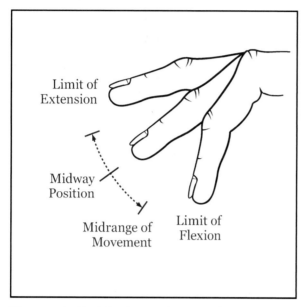

Figure 5A: Positioning and range of movement at the basal joint.

Figure 5B: Positioning and range of movement at the middle joint.

Reason tells us that in learning to play the guitar, training the fingers to operate in the midrange provides optimal leverage or power for the involved muscles thus making the learning process easier, more enjoyable and more rewarding.

Alignment of the Wrist

Fig. 6A shows the proper alignment of the wrist with the side of the basal joint of *i* and the forearm. During early stages of training (until you acquire a secure feeling of alignment) it is helpful to often check this position in a mirror and also to place a ruler (represented by the dotted line) flat along the basal joint, the wrist, and the forearm. Figs. 6B and 6C show incorrect sideways curvatures of the wrist which are recognized as primary causes of crippling

 Repetitive Strain Injury (see the Shearer Online Supplement).

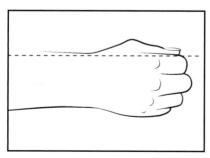 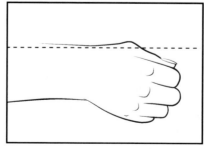 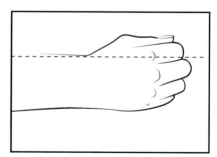

Figure 6A   **Figure 6B**   **Figure 6C**

The Tilt of the Hand

With your hand positioned as shown on p. 2 place the tips of *i*, *m*, *a* on the first three strings half way between the bridge and the end of the fingerboard and rotate your arm counter clockwise so that the tip and middle segments of *i* and *m* are tilted to the left, towards the thumb as shown, in Fig. 7. This is the commonly accepted position for superior tone production and maximum freedom of thumb movement.

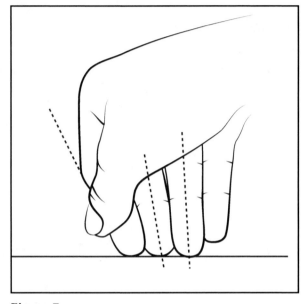

Figure 7

The Optimal Hand Position

We can now understand the optimal position of the hand.

Carefully observe the following:

- The wrist is slightly arched (as in Fig. 4) and aligned with the side of the basal joint of *i*. and the forearm (Fig. 6A).
- The fingers are comfortably flexed in a naturally curved position, approximately midway between full flexion and full extension (Figs. 5A and 5B).
- *P* is positioned straight and resting against the tip joint of *i* (Fig. 4).
- The hand is slightly tilted to the left to provide the simplest, most direct extension and flexion of *p* (Fig. 7).

The Two Kinds of Strokes

The act of sounding a string is called a "stroke." There are two kinds of strokes:

The *Free Stroke* (Spanish *tirando*) occurs when, immediately after sounding a string, *p* or a finger passes freely above the adjacent string in the direction of the movement.

The *Rest Stroke* (Sp. *apoyando*) occurs when, immediately after sounding a string, *p* or a finger comes to rest against the adjacent string in the direction of the movement, except in the case of the sixth string when the direction of movement is maintained as though a lower string were present.

For this book we'll focus solely on *free stroke*.

Reviewing the Strings of the Guitar

Before proceeding, review the strings of the guitar which are indicated with circled numbers—①②③④⑤⑥. The thinnest string ① sounds the highest and the thickest string ⑥ sounds the lowest. This can be confusing because when the guitar is properly positioned, ⑥ lies over the highest part of the soundhole and ① over the lowest part of the soundhole.

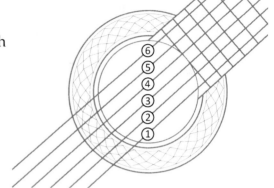

TRAINING THE THUMB (*P*)

We begin right-hand training with *p*. Such an approach results in quickly beginning to play meaningful little pieces while establishing the basis for a secure technique.

First, in order to establish clear aims of positioning and movement before attempting to play, carefully read the following information and thoroughly study the DVD. Carefully observe the hand and *p* while carrying out the following:

- Assume the Optimal Hand Position (described on p.4) and with the right shoulder comfortably relaxed (and the L.H. resting on the left thigh), place the tips of *i* and *m* lightly against ① to stabilize the hand.

- Be sure to maintain the tilt of the hand for the most powerful and free movement of *p*.

- Next, extend *p* at the *P*-B joint (at the wrist) to its comfortable limit of extension and without sounding a string, flex back to *i*; extend and flex directly without swerving while minimizing extension and flexion at the tip joint.

- Practice this movement until you've acquired a feeling of moving from the *P*-B joint as explained in the DVD, then proceed to sound the strings.

Tone Quality and Your Nails

When the guitar is well played, perhaps its most attractive characteristic is its tone. A beautiful tone is achieved by playing with nails. You should begin using your nails as soon as they've grown to an adequate length for effective shaping. Sounding the strings with the nails requires different finger movements from those used when sounding the strings without the nails. By using your nails from the beginning of right-hand study, you'll avoid forming habits which must eventually be replaced. For more information on nails, see the DVD and the online supplement (www.aaronshearerfoundation.org).

Sounding Strings with the Prepared (*P*) Free Stroke

Begin by sounding ③ in the following manner:

- With the finger tips still placed lightly against the first string ① for stability, extend *p* in the same manner as in the preceding exercise and place the left tip of *p* firmly against the third string, as shown in the DVD; pause to be sure the placement of *p* is firm and secure using the nail if possible.
- Then sound string ③ and follow through coming firmly to rest against the tip joint of *i*. Since the pause is in "preparation" for sounding the string, this is called a *prepared free stroke* or simply a *prepared stroke*.
- It's essential to form the prepared-stroke habit from the beginning of training; the following simple approach called the spoken "prep-play" exercise is very useful in acquiring this habit: Say "prep" for the preparation phase and "play" for the sounding/follow-through phase—prep-play, prep-play, etc.—evenly and not too fast.

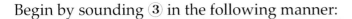

"prep" | "play"   "prep" | "play"   "prep" | "play"   "prep" | "play"   "prep" |
          ③   ③   ③   ③

- Repeat until the movement feels reasonably secure. Then, in the same manner, practice sounding ④. The prepared stroke provides the basis for producing a secure, powerful, full-bodied tone, and is a crucial element of technique.

In beginning R.H. development, a slight pause to execute a prepared stroke is essential, but this results in briefly damping the string producing a *staccato* (disconnected) effect. However, as habits of control and accuracy are acquired, the pause will gradually lessen so that the firm placement becomes automatic and occurs instantly without a pause, thereby resulting in a *legato* (smoothly connected) effect, called *continuity stroke*. Acquiring the habit of executing the prepared stroke is so important that you should practice it several times daily until the movement is secure before proceeding.

Further right-hand training requires the ability to read basic music notation.

BASIC MUSIC NOTATION

Notation is the system of notes and other signs or symbols used in writing music. A written note indicates two basic qualities:

1) *pitch,* or highness or lowness of the note's sound.
2) *rhythm,* or duration of the note.

Pitch is indicated by notes placed on the staff of five lines and four spaces numbered from the bottom upward as shown:

There are seven different notes in the musical alphabet, referred to by letter name—A, B, C, D, E, F, G—or *solfege* name—*do, re, mi, fa, so, la, ti, do.* In this book, you will learn both. For more information on the use of solfege, please visit the Shearer Online Supplement.

Observe the *treble clef* sign placed at the beginning of the staff and that the scroll of this sign encircles the second line of the staff. This second line fixes where the note G (so) is written, the name of the third string of the guitar identified by a number in a circle: ③. The note D (re), the name of string ④ of the guitar, is notated in the space immediately below the staff.

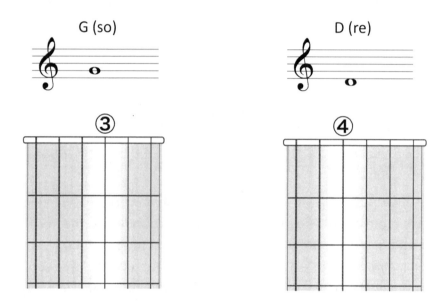

We can understand rhythm by first understanding *beats,* or steady pulses. The beats written on the staff below are called *quarter notes*:

Ex. 1a

Beats are organized into units called *measures* as marked off by *bar lines.* Notice below that there are 2 quarter notes in each measure:

Ex. 1b

The number of beats per measure is indicated by a *time signature* located just to the right of the clef sign. A time signature of $\frac{2}{4}$ means each measure lasts for the time of two quarter notes. Thus, $\frac{2}{4} = \frac{2}{\text{♩}}$

In the example below, count the quarter-note beats in each measure.

Ex.2

If tapping your foot along while counting the beat helps you maintain a steady pulse, do so.

When counting, give emphasis to first beat in each measure. This is the *strong beat* since it begins the measure. The second beat is referred to as the *weak beat*. This grouping of strong to weak beats establishes what is referred to as *meter*. In Ex. 2 the meter is *duple meter*, since it is defined by two beats.

Practicing beats on the guitar

When playing beats on the guitar, it is helpful to use a *metronome*. A metronome is a tool which establishes the speed or *tempo* of your practice. The metronome sounds a steady *tick* which may be adjusted slower or faster as a number of beats per minute. Use these ticks to serve as references for beats (the ticks you hear on the TNT2 Audio represent the beats).

Developing the prepared stroke should be a priority for now. Be sure to practice slowly enough to clearly feel the firmly prepared stroke placement of *p* against the string (see p.6 and DVD 14).

The Half Note: ♩ or ♭

As its name implies, the half note is equivalent to 2 quarter notes and thus receives two counts.

$$\text{𝅗𝅥} = \text{♩} + \text{♩}$$

Count evenly at a moderate tempo (set your metronome to about 60) and practice examples 3a and 3b using carefully executed prepared strokes:

Ex. 3a

Ex. 3b

Beginning to Read and Play Music

You've now acquired the basics to begin reading and playing music on the guitar. Your first pieces are four easy duets containing only G (so), and D (re) and the values 𝅗𝅥 and 𝅘𝅥. Playing them accurately, however, requires carrying out an important procedure before playing, called *Pre-reading*.

BEGINNING PRE-READING

The purpose of pre-reading is to form and clarify your aims[4]—a process that involves *visualization*.[5] You will save much time and develop stronger feelings of security and confidence by thoroughly carrying out the four following steps before attempting to play a piece for the first time.

1. Pre-read one line at a time or less if you feel confused.

2. Scan (closely examine) the piece for anything you don't understand. If you find anything confusing, be sure to clarify it before attempting to play.

3. Begin by setting a tempo for the rhythm. This is extremely important. For the sake of accuracy, choose a tempo that's slower than you think is necessary. Feel the tempo (using a metronome if available) by counting at least a full measure of beats. While counting aloud gently clap the correct duration of each note; thus a quarter note is clapped with no pause, while a half note requires holding the hands together for two counts. Proceed in this manner at a slow enough tempo to feel confident and secure. If you feel insecure, stop and try a slower tempo.

4. Vocalize—say or sing the note's letter or solfege name.

---

[4] If your awareness of the importance of aims is unclear, you should review the paragraphs pertaining to the subject of Aims in the Introduction, pp. xv.

[5] Be certain that the meaning of visualization is clear; if not, you need to review The Natural Abilities to Visualize and Concentrate explained in the Introduction, p. xiv.

5. Once you clarify the name of the note and its rhythm, visualize its location on the guitar. Then say (or sing) its solfege name aloud at the set tempo and visualize the location in your mind's eye where the note is played.

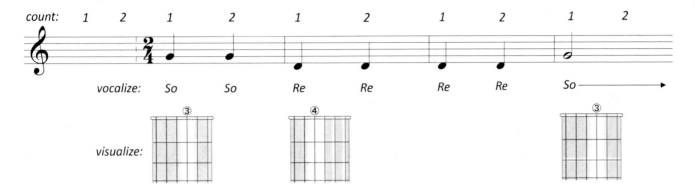

The ease with which you learn to play any piece will depend on how thoroughly and accurately you carry out the pre-reading procedure.

Proceeding to Play and Say

When comfortable with Pre-reading proceed to "Playing and Saying" the selection as demonstrated in this video.

Duets and Using the Multimedia disc

Your first pieces are duets with you playing the upper part, marked **S** for *student* and the *teacher*, marked **T**, or another person playing the lower part. As with <u>all</u> duets in this book, using the accompanying Audio Track is highly recommended and beneficial. The recorded duets include TNT2 software.

Be sure to Pre-Read and Play and Say before playing with the Audio Track. Also remember to maintain firm contact of your nails to the strings with your prepared stroke.

Play I

AUDIO 1

Duet No. 1

Play II

AUDIO 2

Duet No. 2

BEGINNING EXPRESSION IN MUSIC

Expression is the element that gives feeling and a lifelike spirit to music. Simply put, it is the nuance of change that results from the way a performer interprets music. Though expression can be very specifically notated, every performer expresses music somewhat differently. Thus, the most effective and rewarding study of expression requires the guidance of a teacher and in my opinion should start as early as possible in one's musical study.

Expressive markings are used beginning with the following duet, *Play III,* which introduces *dynamics.* Dynamics are the levels of loudness and softness, notated by markings below the staff. To begin, we will use the following symbols which like most are Italian in origin:

f for *forte* (pronounced *for*tay) meaning "loud."

p for *piano,* meaning "quiet."

Music can be played *forte* or *piano,* but often there is a smooth change from one dynamic to the next. This is commonly shown with wedges, indicating *crescendo* (gradually louder) or *decrescendo* (gradually softer).

crescendo

decrescendo

Before playing *Play III,* repeatedly practice the changes from *piano* to *forte* on ③:

For more information on Musical Expression, see the Shearer Online Supplement.

Play III

Duet No. 3

Play IV

Duet No. 4

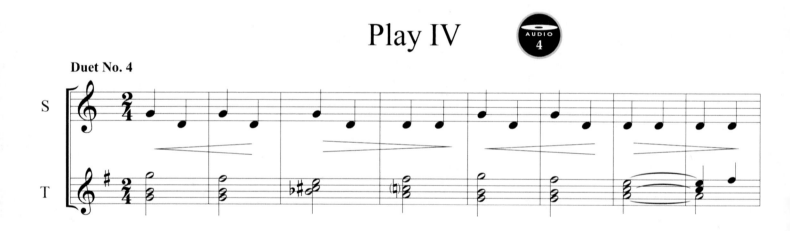

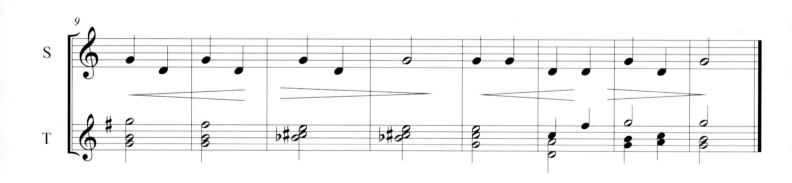

$\frac{4}{4}$ OR COMMON TIME AND THE WHOLE NOTE

The $\frac{4}{4}$ time signature means that each measure has the time of 4 quarter notes.

Since it is so commonly used, it is referred to as *common time,* often notated with the symbol: $\mathbf{C}$
When counting, beats <u>1</u> and <u>3</u> are strong and beats <u>2</u> and <u>4</u> are weak.

As its name implies, the whole note **o** is equivalent to two half notes and therefore receives
four counts, or the time of one complete measure as in Ex. 4.

Count and clap Ex. 4, keeping your hands together for the full duration of the half and whole
notes. Be sure to stress the strong beats.

Ex. 4

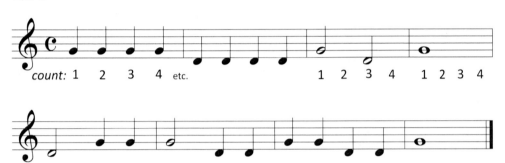

The Open Second String

The name of the open (o) second string ② is B (ti—pronounced *tee*) and is notated on the third
line of the staff:

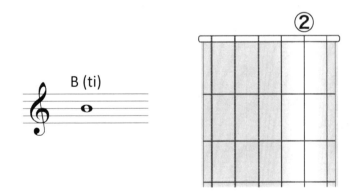

Visualize the ③-②-③-④ pattern of Ex. 5 before playing, and then carefully watch *p* while you play (slowly at first) to be certain that:

- You're firmly preparing the stroke with the nail against the string (if possible).
- Extension and flexion is occurring at the *P-B* joint.
- You're directly following through, coming to rest against the tip-joint of *i*.

Ex. 5

Carefully visualize and pre-read Ex. 6 before playing.

Ex. 6

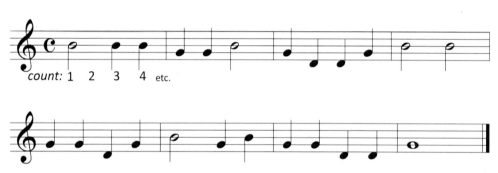

Carefully pre-read and visualize *Hornpipe* before playing. Work one line at a time.

Hornpipe

Solo No. 1

RESTS IN MUSIC

The most fundamental of all musical elements are sounds, notated by *notes* and silences notated by *rests*. A rest is notated by a sign indicating the duration of silence of the note it replaces—for example: a *quarter rest* equals the duration of a quarter note, a *half rest* equals the duration of a half note, etc. (For more information about rest signs in music, see www.aaronshearerfoundation.org).

The Quarter Rest: (𝄽)

The quarter rest 𝄽 is counted as one beat. When counting and clapping notes and rests, hold the hands together for the duration of a note and apart for the duration of a rest.

Ex. 7

Counting Duet I

Duet No. 5

The Half Rest: (-)

Ex. 8

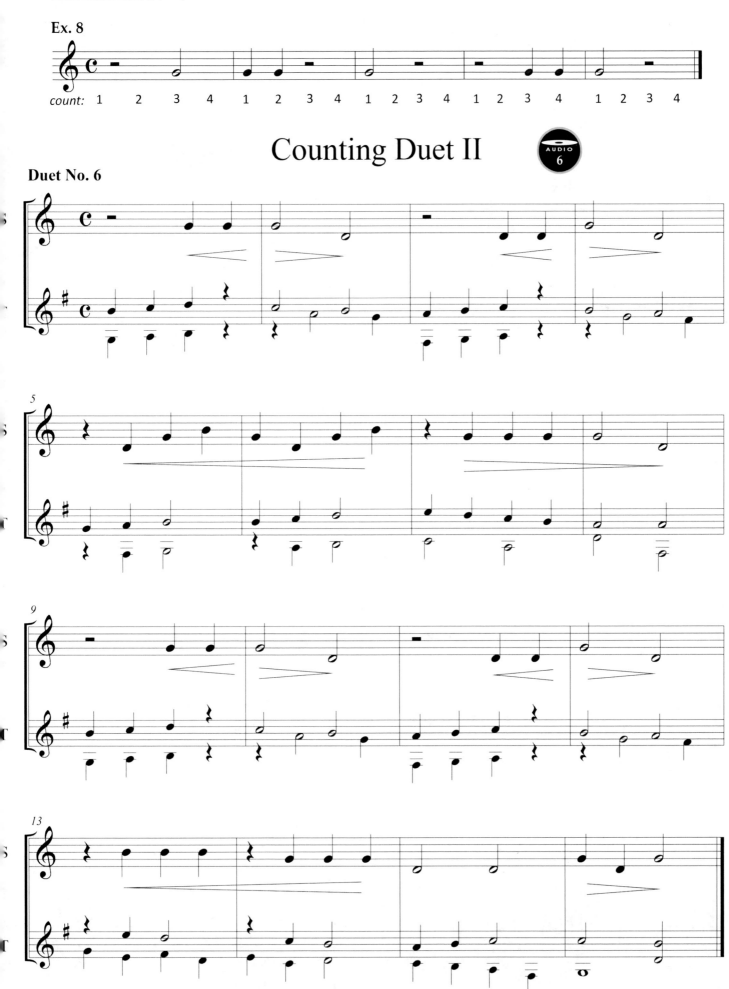

count: 1 2 3 4 1 2 3 4 1 2 3 4 1 2 3 4 1 2 3 4

Counting Duet II

Duet No. 6

The Whole Rest: (-)

Ex. 9

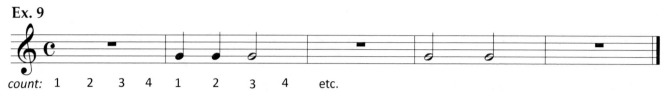

count: 1 2 3 4 1 2 3 4 etc.

Counting Duet III

Duet No. 7

At the beginning of Duet No. 8, the marking, **M.M.** ♩ = 100 indicates that your metronome should be set to 100, meaning 100 beats per minute. This is a goal tempo, a speed that you should ultimately be able to perform with security.

Duet No. 8

Counting Duet IV

Beginning Notes on the Fingerboard and Left-Hand Training

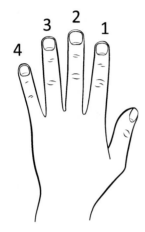

The left-hand fingers are identified by the Arabic numbers: 1, (index), 2, (middle), 3, (ring) and 4, (little finger) and the left thumb does not require special identification.

Figure 8

The guitar, frets are identified by Roman numerals: I, II, III, IV

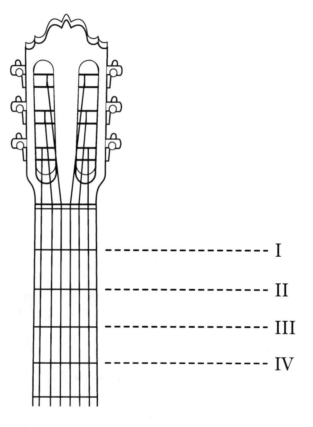

LEFT-HAND OPTIMAL POSITION

Before proceeding:

- Be sure that the L.H. nails are clipped short and neatly shaped to avoid touching the strings or the fingerboard.
- You should carefully review Checking the Left Hand under The Procedure for Positioning the Guitar, p.1, and the DVD 4.
- To achieve the optimal Left-Hand Position, make sure your fingers are in their relaxed midrange position and that your thumb is relaxed and relatively centered behind fingers 1 and 2.

The Note A (la)

Your first note on the fingerboard is A (la) played on ③ at fret II. Be sure your left-hand thumb is optimally positioned behind the neck and centered behind fingers 1 and 2. Place the fingertip of 2 close to the fret and press only firmly enough to obtain a clear tone as demonstrated in the DVD.

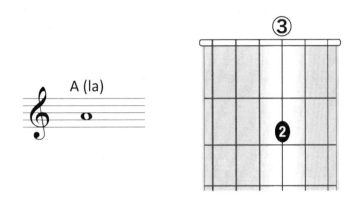

Practice each measure in Ex. 10 separately until secure. Notice in 10c. the left-hand fingering with a horizontal dash (2-). This indicates that the 2nd finger will remain held.

Ex. 10

PRE-READING—SYLLABIC CUE AND *AIR-GUITAR*

With the introduction of notes on the fingerboard, come additional procedures for pre-reading. First of all, when you say (or sing) a note, it now functions as a *syllabic cue*—a mental reminder that prompts a clear visualization of the string/fret/finger combination involved in that note's formation. For example, in vocalizing A (la—pron. *lah*), you should clearly visualize the note on string ③ at fret II formed with finger 2 as explained in the DVD.

Further, it's now beneficial to add the well-known procedure called *Air-Guitar* to your regular routine of study. *Air-Guitar*, should be somewhat self -explanatory. It involves placing the arms, hands and rest of the body in a position as though holding the guitar (though not actually holding it) and either counting or naming the printed notes aloud while visualizing and moving the fingers as though playing. Practicing *air-guitar* greatly clarifies and accelerates the important process of visualization. Those who are willing to slowly and patiently apply it, will find great benefit (see the DVD).

The Repeat Sign

The repeat sign 𝄇 directs you to repeat back to the beginning of a piece and play through it one more time. The repeat is used in the following Duet No. 9, *Smooth Sailing.*

Pre-read one line at a time and then play.

Smooth Sailing

Duet No. 9

In *Dance of Four* notice the 2- at mm. 9 and 13, indicating that finger 2 be held on the A (la).

Dance of Four

Solo No. 2

FURTHER LEFT-HAND TRAINING

The Notes on ②

Form C (do) and D (re) on ②.

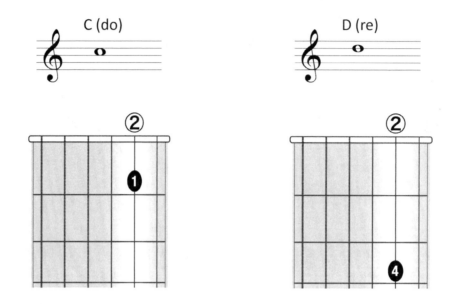

Carefully practice each figure in Ex. 11:

- Be sure your guitar is positioned high enough and far enough to the right for easiest access to these notes with the left hand.
- Refer to DVD 10, to establish the Optimal Hand Position (see pp.2-4).
- First watch as you carefully place the finger to form each note. Then close your eyes, visualize the movement, and play each figure several times.
- In playing the successive C-D sequence which appears in all four figures, gently hold 1 (indicated with a dash: 1-) on C as you form D with 4. This helps to provide a feeling of security during the movement, as well as a legato (smoothly connected) sound.

Ex. 11

TEMPO EXPRESSION

So far, you have learned to express the musical dynamics. Now you will begin to express nuances of *tempo*, that is, the speed of musical beats.

- *rit.* is the abbreviation for *ritardando* (reetardahndo) which means to gradually slow down. This is used when approaching the end of a phrase or end of a piece.
- *a tempo* (ah tempoh), meaning to return to the original tempo, is often used following the *rit.*

Unlike dynamic markings, *tempo* markings are generally placed above the music. To develop a sense of tempo expression, practice the following.

Be sure you can fluently pre-read each new piece, including all expressive terms, before attempting to play.

REPEAT ENDINGS IN MUSIC

The following Duet No. 10, *Step and Skip* introduces new repeat notation. First, there is a *forward facing repeat sign* 𝄆 at m. 9 which marks the point to where you repeat. Thus after playing m.16, repeat to m. 9, and not to the beginning of the piece. The second time through, skip m. 16 and go directly to m. 17. These two measures are called *repeat endings*, specifically *1st* and *2nd endings*.

Before playing *Step and Skip* and *Scale Song*, be sure to pre-read and visualize one phrase at a time.

Step and Skip

Duet No. 10

Scale Song

Solo No. 3

$\frac{3}{4}$ TIME AND THE DOTTED-HALF NOTE: (𝅗𝅥.)

The $\frac{3}{4}$ time signature means that each measure consists of the time of 3 quarter notes and is counted 1, 2, 3. The dotted-half note introduces an important rule that applies in all music notation: a dot following a note increases it's time by one half. Thus, a dotted half equals the time of 1 half note plus 1 quarter note.

$$𝅗𝅥. = 𝅗𝅥 + 𝅘𝅥$$

Since there are 2 quarter notes in each half, a dotted-half note also equals the time of 3 quarter notes

$$𝅗𝅥. = 𝅘𝅥 + 𝅘𝅥 + 𝅘𝅥$$

$\frac{3}{4}$ is also referred to as *triple meter* since there are three beats in each measure. The 1st beat is *strong* and beats 2 and 3 are *weak*. Practice this new meter in Ex. 12 by counting aloud while softly clapping each note. Use a metronome or if it helps you to maintain a steady beat, tap your foot lightly. Remember to hold the hands together for the full duration of each note:

Ex. 12

count: 1   2   3   1   2   3   etc.

Duet No. 11

Tripla

Skipping Lightly

Solo No. 4

Waltz Tune

Solo No. 5

Gliding Along

Solo No. 6

Summit

Duet No. 12

M.M. ♩ = 75

Beginning Training the R.H. Fingers

Free Stroke with I-M

ESSENTIALS FOR BEGINNING R.H. FINGER TRAINING

We began R.H. training with *p* free stroke because it's easier than beginning with rest stroke. It's for the same reason that we begin training the R.H. fingers with free stroke.

- Be sure you understand how to form clear aims; if in doubt, do not proceed without thoroughly reviewing the Introduction, (pp.xiii-xvii).

- It's essential that you can identify the R.H. fingers by their letter names: *i, m, a, c,* and the names of the finger joints: basal, middle, and tip, (pp.1-2).

- You should be able to visualize and describe the relationship between Optimal Hand Position, Midrange of Joint Movement, and Maximum Leverage for the involved muscles, (p.2 and DVD 10).

- Further, you need to have a clear visualized image of the recommended tilt of the hand and the slightly arched and properly aligned position of the wrist, (p.4 and DVD 9).

BEGINNING FREE STROKE WITH FINGERS

Free stroke with a finger means that after sounding a string, the fingertip passes freely above the adjacent lower string.

It is easier to begin free stroke by sounding two notes together on two adjacent strings (a dyad)[6] with *i* and *m* than by sounding a single note with one finger. There are two main reasons why this approach works well: the first reason is that using the two fingers together ensures proper placement of the hand and fingers; the second reason is that adjacent fingers naturally tend to move together in the same direction of flexion and extension. Thus beginning free stroke with the two naturally best coordinated fingers, *i-m*, results in feelings of greater ease and security in beginning free-stroke training.

Before attempting to actually sound the strings, you can acquire a general idea of the correct free-stroke movement with the fingers through carrying out a common "scratching" motion on the back of your left hand. This will establish an all-important visualized aim for playing free stroke with the fingers on the guitar. Proceed as follows:

- Carefully assume the familiar Optimal Hand Position and place the tips (and nails) of *i, m,* and *p* on the back of the left hand (for R.H. stability), with *a* and *c* flexed slightly past *m*, as shown in the DVD, (see p. 4).

- The basal joints of the fingers should be in their midrange position with the middle

---

[6] The term dyad is used here to identify two notes in close vertical proximity sounded together. Although not as familiar as the common musical term, triad, the clarity and conciseness of dyad would seem to suggest that it be used when applicable.

joints approximately perpendicular to the finger tips.

- Then flex *i* and *m* together mainly at their middle joints along with minimal flexion at the basal joint to gently scratch the back of your hand, touching it only during flexion. The side of *i* should lightly brush against *p* while *a-c* remain slightly flexed and moving along with *i-m* in a well pronounced follow-through.

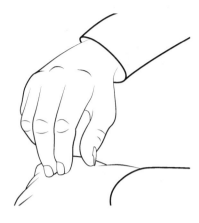

- Observe that most of the movement occurs at the middle joint while the tip and basal joints automatically flex and extend slightly along with the middle joint.

- Check often to maintain the Optimal Hand Position with the wrist properly arched and aligned and the hand tilted during finger movement.

Sounding Strings ③ and ② Free Stroke with *I-M* Together

- When first sounding strings, it's essential to use the prepared stroke to develop a clear and powerful stroke.

- Now on the guitar, place *p* against ④ to steady the hand while using the preceding "scratching" motion to sound ③ and ② with *i-m*, being sure to carefully prepare each stroke before sounding the strings, using the same spoken prep-play procedure as you did with *p* earlier (p.6).

Ex. 13

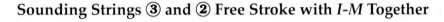

PRE-READING DYADS

You will now use this newly acquired technique of *i-m* together in free stroke to play two simultaneous notes called *dyads*. As always, before you begin on the guitar, clarify your goals by pre-reading using the air-guitar and playing and saying the example.

- Pre-reading now involves vocalizing and visualizing both notes of a dyad. Begin as slowly as necessary to avoid hesitating and say the lower syllable just before the upper syllable, so that the upper syllable falls precisely on the beat as demonstrated in the DVD.

- When you can do this slowly and evenly, say only the higher of the two notes, which will serve as a syllabic cue for clearly visualizing the complete dyad without rhythmic interruption.

- Proceed slowly; then "Play and Say" the example and check, first one hand and then the other, to maintain optimal positions and movements of both. Cultivate the habit of frequent review to achieve feelings of security and ease—the marks of true progress.

 For more information on *Visualization* visit the Shearer Online Supplement.

 ## MOVEMENT FORMS AND ISOLATIONS

Working with dyads brings new demands and challenges to the left hand. When learning a dyad, it is important to visualize its shape or pattern on the fingerboard. The main technical challenge is moving one pattern to the next, which is called a *movement form.*

When guitarists play, they are actually performing a series of movement forms both in the left and right hands. Many movement forms are rather easy and are considered to be part of your vocabulary of movement forms; while others are more difficult and require special attention to become fluent in their use—just like new vocabulary words. If you encounter a movement form which is difficult and outside your vocabulary, then *isolate* it by focusing on the problem. Through careful and thoughtful repetition of the individual movement form, you'll be able to successfully execute the passage.

In Ex. 14, mm. 4-5 might present a challenge in using the 4th finger to play the D on the second string. With this challenge recognized, proceed to isolate the movement form as demonstrated on the DVD.

Ex. 14

Simple Songs I & II provide practice in reading and playing dyads. Do not neglect the right hand preparation and follow-through. Be sure to position the right hand over the strings to maintain an Optimal Position of Leverage for the fingers in free stroke. Measure 6 might present a challenge in adding the 4th finger to play D on ②. Visualize and isolate the excerpt repeatedly until fluent.

Simple Song I

Duet No. 13

rit. . . . .

Simple Song II

Duet No. 14

*⌢ is a *fermata,* which indicates to hold out the duration

THE NOTES ON ①

Notes on ①, E, F, and G, are shown below. Carefully visualize their location on the staff as well as the Optimal L.H. Position for forming these notes which is similar to that for notes on ②.

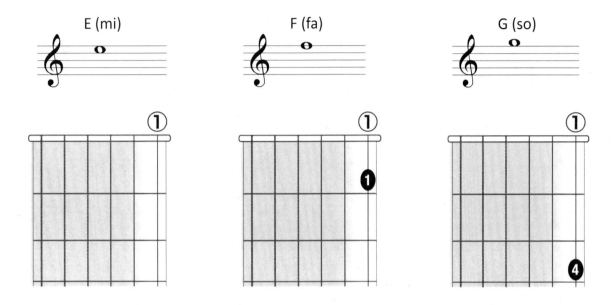

Touch with your left hand and vocalize the following:

Ex. 15a

mi   mi   mi   fa   fa   fa   etc.

Duet No. 15, *Simple Song III,* applies these new notes in dyads. To prepare, first visualize and practice Ex. 15b. Be sure your guitar is positioned high enough and far enough to the right for easiest access to these notes with the left hand.[7]

Ex. 15b

---

[7] This is a main purpose of the Classic Guitar Strap. Don't hesitate to experiment!

Simple Song III

Duet No. 15

SPECIAL TRAINING OF THE LEFT ARM, HAND AND FINGERS

So far in your training, your left hand and arm have remained in a stationary position, enabling security for learning notes. However, there are many instances when the hand/arm must move fluidly in and out of this posture to accommodate certain combinations of fingers on the fingerboard. Such is the case when two notes are formed at the same fret on adjacent strings. Consider the D-G dyad:

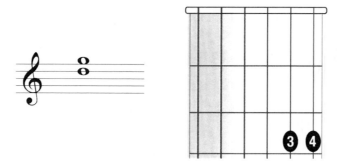

Normally the 4th finger plays D, but in certain instances, 3 plays D and 4 plays G.

Another consideration is the dyad C-F:

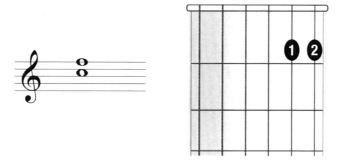

In both cases, pivoting on the finger on the lower adjacent string, slightly rotates the left hand/arm outward from the neck and allows room for the finger on the upper adjacent string. Observe the following directives before playing Ex. 16:

- With 1st finger touching C on ②, lift your left elbow somewhat sideways away from your body so that the wrist and forearm slightly rotate clockwise and the right side of your palm is well away from the edge of the fingerboard.
- Place 2 on F on ①, while keeping 1 on ②.
- Release 2 on ①, rotating the wrist and forearm back to the normal playing position, keeping the middle and tip joints well flexed to provide leverage for pressing the strings firmly against the frets.

Ex. 16

ACCIDENTALS

Pitches may be adjusted slightly higher or lower using *accidentals*. An accidental may be a sharp (♯) which raises the sound by one fret or a flat (♭) which lowers the sound by one fret. Your first accidental is C♯ used in *Simple Song IV*. Its location is on ② at fret II, one fret above C.

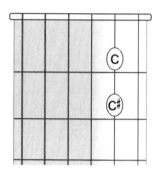

 Since the accidental slightly changes the pitch, we solfege with a modified syllable. Rather than saying *do-sharp* we simply brighten the vowel and say *di* (dee). **IMPORTANT**: The sharp sign affects the note for the entire measure in which it appears and only in that measure.

Remember to pre-read *Simple Song IV*, isolating any challenging left-hand shapes and/or movement forms.

Simple Song IV

Duet No. 16

THE TIE AND F♯ ON ①

The following duet, *Simple Song V*, introduces a few new considerations. First of all, the *tie* is a curved line connecting two consecutive notes of the same pitch. Notes connected by a tie are counted no differently but have added duration. In the excerpt below, 3rd beat dyad, C-E is tied across the bar line to the 1st beat. Be sure when counting and clapping that you keep your hands together for the duration of the tie as demonstrated in the video.

count: 1   2   3   1   2   3

As shown above, tying the 3rd beat creates a rhythmic stress not natural for triple meter. This new stress or *accent* on weak beat 3 is indicated by the accent mark: (>) which means to play louder.

Notice also the new accidental—F♯ or fi (fee):

F♯ (fi)

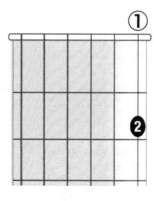

Simple Song V

Duet No. 17

AUDIO 17

RIGHT-HAND STRING CROSSING

The preceding pieces have afforded ease and security using different length right-hand fingers to sound pairs of strings. For example, the longer finger *m*, reaches ①, while the shorter finger *i* reaches ②. Organizing the right hand this way allows each finger to function in its Optimal Midrange Position.

In pieces where changing to different string pairs occur, the R.H. (and arm) must be moved up or down from the elbow to maintain the same string/finger relationship to each pair of strings. This technique is called *string crossing* (see www.aaronshearerfoundation.org).

Consider the following:

- Since crossing to an adjacent pair of strings involves a relatively subtle movement from the elbow joint—the short distance of one string to the next—developing accuracy requires a clear aim and thoughtful practice.

- Crossing from the ②-③ pair to the ①-② pair and vice versa in Exs. 17a & b should be practiced until the visualized aim and feel of the crossing movement are clear.

- As a temporary aid, markings ②③ or ①② will be placed above the staff indicating to what string pair a crossing is to be made.

- First watch the crossing movement using the air-guitar, then close your eyes and practice achieving the feeling of midrange finger movement for sounding the different pairs of strings.

Ex. 17a

Ex. 17b

Breeze

Duet No. 18

M.M. ♩ = 75

Solo Playing of Music in Two Parts

ALTERNATING *P* FREE STROKE WITH FINGERS FREE STROKE

You will now approach fuller sounding solo pieces consisting of two parts: an upper treble part alternating with a lower bass part. Notes in the treble part with stems up are sounded with fingers; bass notes with stems down are sounded with *p*.

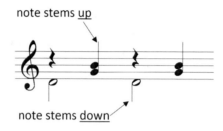

Playing music of this type means that when *p* flexes, fingers extend; when fingers flex, *p* extends. Consequently you'll no longer have the constant steadying support of *p* on a lower string, or a finger on a higher string. Instead, support will result from the proper timing and preparation of the *p*/finger alternation.

Proceed as follows:

- Move only the fingers and *p*; the arm should be kept steady with the wrist slightly arched to retain the optimal hand position.
- Be sure to establish and maintain the feeling of a secure prepared stroke with both the fingers and *p*.
  - □ prepare *i-m* when sounding *p*.
  - □ prepare *p* when *i-m* sounds.
- To help clarify the rhythm of music in two parts, you should use the "two-hand tap" during pre-reading: tap the upper part with the right hand on the right thigh, while tapping the lower part with the left hand on the left thigh.
- Then proceed to take your right hand to the soundboard of the guitar:
  - □ tap the bass line with the thumb
  - □ tap the stem-up line with *i, m, a, c,* fingers.
  - □ count and tap the following:

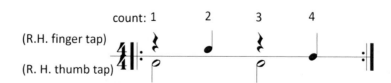

This method of tapping on the soundboard is highly beneficial as a means to work out any rhythmic challenge involving *p* and the fingers.

Note: With the previous support of the right hand now missing, counterproductive tension may develop in the shoulder muscles sometimes resulting in soreness and even severe pain. To avoid acquiring this harmful and possibly crippling habit of shoulder tension a conscious effort is required to relax the entire shoulder area in beginning this training (see the Shearer Online Supplement).

Ex. 18a and *Alternating Study I & II* all incorporate a half note on beats 3 and 4 to allow ample time for the thumb and ultimately the fingers to prepare (see the DVD).

Ex. 18a

Alternating Study I

Solo No. 7

* rest *p* lightly against tip of *i*

Alternating Study II

Solo No. 8

* rest *p* lightly against tip of *i*

ALTERNATION OF *P* AND TWO FINGERS (*I-M*) WITHOUT PAUSE

When comfortable with the alternation of *p* and *i-m*, progress to performing it without pause as in Ex. 18b. Remember as *i-m* sound, *p* prepares; and as *p* sounds, *i-m* prepares. Be sensitive to any counterproductive tension that might develop in the shoulder.

Ex. 18b

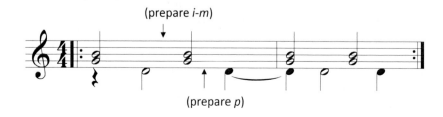

Alternating Study III

Solo No. 9

Alternating Study IV introduces G♯ (si) on ③. Remember, an accidental affects all of the same recurring note within the measure. Thus, in m. 20 all G's are sharped.

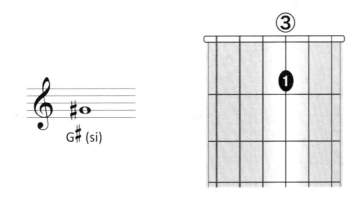

G♯ (si)

Alternating Study IV

Solo No. 10

Music Box

Solo No. 11

THE OPEN STRINGS ⑤ AND ⑥

Strings ④, ⑤, & ⑥ are called "wound" strings because they are made by winding light gauge metal wire around a core of spun synthetic material. This clearly distinguishes these three strings from the higher three strings which are made of solid synthetic material. The three wound strings are commonly referred to as the bass strings or "basses" while the three higher strings are called the treble strings or "trebles."

Two new basses, E ⑥ and A ⑤, sound so low that notating them requires extension lines, or *ledger lines*, below the staff. The note A (la) — ⑤ is notated on the second ledger line and E (mi) — ⑥ is notated below the third ledger line:

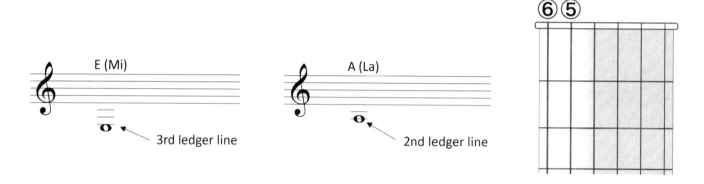

In learning to play these strings, place *i* and *m* on ③ and ② to support the hand. This permits *p*, in sounding ⑤ and ⑥ to move in a similar manner as before in sounding ②, ③, and ④.

Pre-reading should include saying syllables aloud no faster than will permit the clear visualization of each string on the guitar and, if necessary, also saying the string number.

Free Stylin'

Duet No. 19

HARMONICS

The guitar is capable of producing a variety of interesting effects and colors. One of the easiest of these is the *harmonic*. Harmonics are beautiful bell-like sounds made by lightly touching at very specific points along the string. They sound higher than normal notes and are written with special diamond-head notation. For additional information on harmonics visit the on-line supplement.

For beginners the easiest place to play a harmonic is at fret XII.
Starting with ①:

- With L.H. finger 2 or 3, lightly touch the string directly above the XII fret, without depressing the string against the fret.
- Sound the string firmly with *p* midway between the edge of the soundhole and the bridge.
- Remove the L.H. finger as soon as the harmonic begins to sound.
- Repeat this procedure on strings ②, ③, ④, ⑤, and ⑥.

Executing clean sounding harmonics requires developing sensitivity to the timing of the fingers. Touching the string too long and/or removing the finger too soon are common mistakes. When you feel secure sounding harmonics, practice reading them.

There are a variety of ways to notate harmonics. For ease of use in this book, harmonics will be shown as open string, diamond-head notes with a Roman numeral indicating which fret to be played. At fret XII, harmonics actually sound 8 pitches higher (octave) than where written. Read and play the following:

B♭ on ③

The following duet, *Petite Valse II* includes a harmonic as the final note and introduces the note B♭, formed on ③ at III.

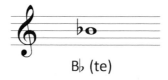

B♭ (te)

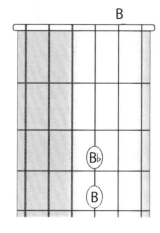

Recall that a flat (♭) lowers the pitch of a note by one fret. Since B is an open string, lowering its pitch isn't possible. However, every note on the guitar has more than one address on the fingerboard. B may also be formed on ③ at IV which when lowered to fret III changes to B♭.

Pre-read and practice this exercise with B♭ — sound the string with your thumb.

Pre-read and practice these dyads with *i-m*.

For expressive purposes, from this Audio Track forward you will notice the omission of the metronome.

Petite Valse II

Duet No. 20

NOTES ON THE STRING ④

Notes on the string ④ include E (mi) at II and F (fa) at III.

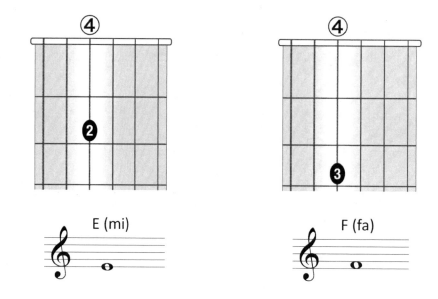

Play the following with *p*, placing *i* and *m* on strings ③ & ② to steady the right hand.

Ex. 19

Continue playing with *p*, place *i* and *m* on ① & ② and practice notes on ④ & ③ including the B♭. Remember to thoroughly visualize and perform the entire example.

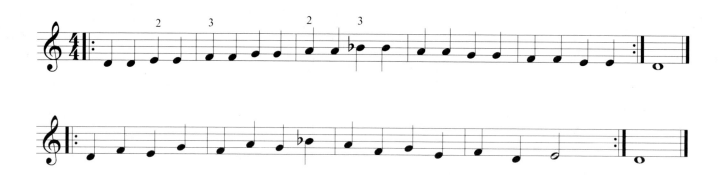

Prelude in Minor

Duet No. 21

Beginning Arpeggios: Sympathetic Movement

The startling speed with which notes are sometimes heard to cascade from the classic guitar is likely to be an instance of a virtuoso performing music consisting of arpeggios or broken chords. This is an example of the highly developed natural functioning of the mind and hands, called *sympathetic movement*, which results in seemingly effortless expressive power and speed.

Now that you've developed security alternating *p* and *i-m* free stroke, you're ready to begin training with *arpeggios*. The word arpeggio comes from the Italian *arpeggiare* which means "to play on the harp." On the guitar this translates to playing a group of at least three notes in succession.

SYMPATHETIC MOVEMENT

As you know, the two notes of a dyad are sounded precisely together. But dyads played in a context of an arpeggio are played one after the other using *sympathetic movement*. The word *sympathetic* pertains to the innate attraction or pull a flexing finger has on an adjacent finger. In the case of *i* and *m*, when *i* flexes *m* is pulled sympathetically. To understand this, study the following text and the DVD.

It is easiest to begin this training with *i-m* sounding ③ and ② as follows:

- Study the DVD to form clear aims.
- Place *p* on ⑤ to support the hand in the Optimal Right Hand Position (see p.4).
- Together, "prepare" *i* on ③ and *m* on ② in position for playing free stroke. (The inactive fingers *a* and *c* should be kept loosely flexed past *m*).
- Firmly flex *i* to sound ③ so that you feel a sympathetic pull on *m* which flexes, sounds ② and follows through along with *i* (*a* & *c* move with *m*). Deliberately repeat this movement until you can clearly feel the sympathetic follow through of *m*.

SYMPATHETIC MOVEMENT IN ARPEGGIOS: P, I, M

Training begins with the *p, i, m* arpeggio because it is the simplest form of sympathetic movement. One of your most central aims in this exercise should be to develop controlled timing of the sympathetic movement between *i* and *m*. This is very closely related to the movement used in sounding dyads, and should feel similar. Be sure to proceed slowly and with clear aims; with careful work you will develop habits of control and evenness that will benefit your playing substantially.

Carry out the following:

- Place *p* against ④, *i* against ③, and *m* against ②, while *a* and *c* remain slightly flexed past *m*.
- Play each string in succession, starting with *p*, moving *a* and *c* along with *m*, and being sure to maintain an even rhythm.
- Notice the slight pull that *i* exerts on *m*.
- During the rest, prepare *p*.
- Then when *p* sounds, simultaneously prepare *i-m*.
- Be sure to maintain the same prepared approach to free stroke you have been using thus far.

Ex. 20

Da Capo

As you pre-read *Etude in G*, you'll notice the word *Fine* (Italian, pron. fee-fay) at the end of the 4th line and *D.C. al Fine* marked over the last measure. D.C stands for *da capo* (pron. dah-cah-poh) –" to the head," *al Fine*—"until the end." Thus, D.C. al Fine means *repeat to the beginning of the piece until the end* (marking).

Etude in G

Solo No. 12

CHORDS

Arpeggio pieces such as *Etude in G* involve reading patterns referred to as *chords*. By definition, chords are groups of three or more notes which sound either simultaneously or as an arpeggio. Many chords are easy to play on the guitar and are named by a letter and quality such as C *major* or A *minor*. The *major* quality can be described as sounding bright (happy) and the *minor* quality as sounding dark (sad).[8]

When learning chords, it's helpful to first visualize their shapes on the fingerboard. In the next solo, *Etude in C*, there are four chords that recur throughout. They are shown below in both fingerboard diagrams and music notation:

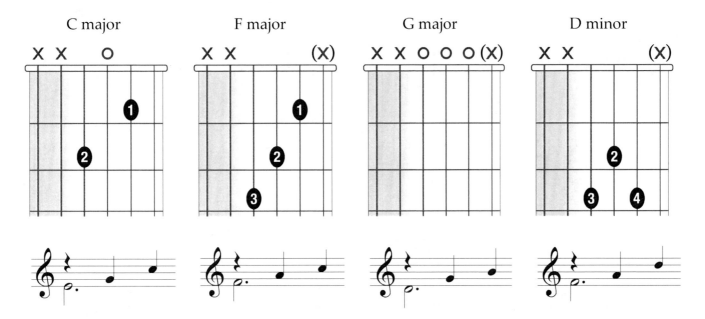

Notice the particular shapes associated with each of the chords. F major appears as "stepladder" shape, while the D minor appears as a "triangle."

Each chord may be sounded with a *strum*, carried out by gently moving the right-hand thumb across the strings from lowest to highest. When strumming, do not include strings marked with an "x." However, for now, you may include string ① marked with an (x) for ease of strumming. This is to show that its pitch is not "officially" part of the chord.

After thoroughly familiarizing yourself with each chord, practice moving between different chords. For the time being, chords will be notated in rhythm only with their name shown above the staff.

- this symbol ⟋ indicates a strum for the duration of one quarter note.
- indicating a strum for the duration of the half note, is the symbol ⟋.
- this symbol ⟋ indicates a strum for the duration of a whole note.

When reading chords in music, names are often shortened. With just its letter name, the chord quality is understood as major. For example C means C major. A lowercase "m" following the letter means the chord is minor. For example, *Dm* means D minor.

---

[8] For more information on chords and harmony see *Classic Guitar Technique Supplement 2* by Aaron Shearer or *The Complete Idiot's Guide to 30 Classical Guitar Favorites* by Thomas Kikta, both published by Alfred Publishing.

Practice strumming and moving between C and F chords. Begin by watching your fingers on the fingerboard, to help guide them into their frets. As you feel more secure, try moving from chord to chord without watching:

Now practice the same procedure between C and Dm chords:

When you feel secure with the chords in the exercises above, proceed to *Etude in C.* As always, be sure to pre-read and visualize .

SYMPATHETIC MOVEMENT IN ARPEGGIOS: P, I, M WITHOUT PAUSE

The *p, i, m* arpeggio is most frequently played without a pause. You must learn to evenly connect the preparation of the thumb and fingers while moving with continuity. Proceed as follows:

- As *p* sounds its string and follows through, prepare the fingers;
- as *m* moves sympathetically with *i* to sound its string, *p* extends and prepares for its next stroke.

Moving the *p,i,m* with continuity takes time and patience—always be sure to practice using prepared stroke until secure.

Ex. 21

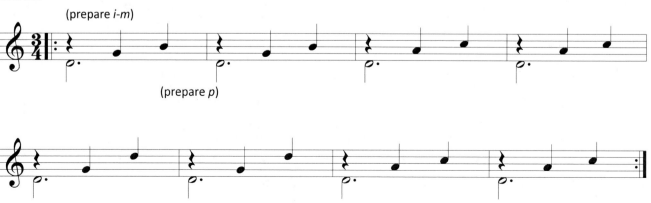

Etude in C

Solo No. 13

THE INDEFINITE TIE AND *SIMILE*

You have already learned that a tie connects the durations of one note to another. There is another kind of tie, the *indefinite tie*, which is used when a note is permitted to continue sounding beyond its normal duration. This is often used to indicate holding a finger for a prolonged period, thereby producing longer sustain.

The example below is from *Flowing*, Solo No. 14. Notice that *p* plays A (la) marked with indefinite ties. Keeping 2 on A (la) allows it to continue sounding throughout two measures.

The marking *simile* (m. 3) means that you should continue expressing in the manner already established. Specifically, it means the G#'s should be sustained as if marked with indefinite ties. *Simile* applies to all similar measure throughout the piece.

Flowing uses the already familiar notes E (mi), A (la), and D (re) with *p*. In addition, notice the harmonic dyads at mm.31 & 48. These should be played with *i* & *m*. Be sure to pre-read carefully, counting the rhythms before you begin playing.

D.S al Fine

Flowing uses the *D.S. al Fine* marking which is similar to *D.C al Fine*. *D.S.* stands for *dal Segno* (pron. dahl sayn-noh) meaning "to the sign." Thus, *D.S. al Fine* means to repeat to the sign (𝄋) and then play to the end (*fine*).

Flowing

Solo No. 14

KEY SIGNATURE

When first approaching a piece of music, it's important to know what *key* it has been written in. The *key* tells us something about the piece's musical environment, or setting. This is as simple as realizing that there is an important note and/or chord which the piece centers around and begins and ends on. This note or chord provides a sense of musical *home,* since so much of the music seems to return to it.

The key is indicated by a *key signature*[9] which appears as a grouping of sharps or flats at the beginning of each music staff.

key signature

The excerpt above is from Duet No. 22, *Boat Song.* Notice the key signature of two sharps—F♯ and C♯ which appear between the treble clef and the time signature. These sharps are understood as fixtures throughout the piece, meaning that F's and C's must be realized as F♯'s and C♯'s. This applies to <u>all</u> F's and C's, no matter where they are written.

THE KEY OF D MAJOR

The key of two sharps is called *D major,* which has a *home note* of D and a *home chord* of D major. This chord along with the A major are frequent patterns used in *Boat Song.*

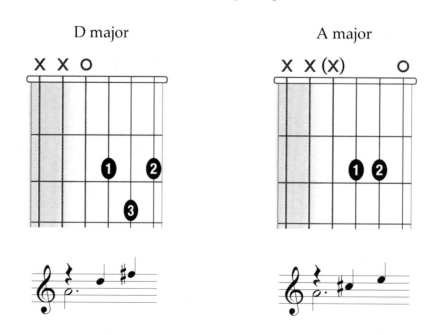

---

[9] A thorough understanding of keys, key signatures, and other elements of the way music is written is essential for learning to play the guitar well. See my *Basic Elements of Music Theory for the Guitar* Alfred Publishing

Notice D and A chords share a *common note*/finger—the note A on ③. Keeping 1 on ③ when switching from one chord to the next, helps to connect the sound. Practice strumming the D and A chords:

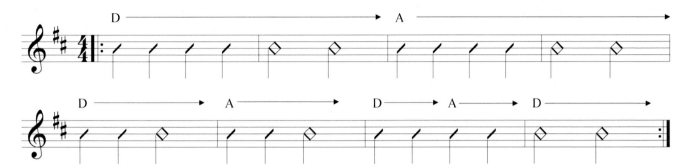

Boat Song actually uses a simpler 2-finger version of the D chord. However, in the context of moving from A to D chord, it may feel more comfortable to leave 1- on ③, making the D chord look and feel as its fuller form (see below).

D major

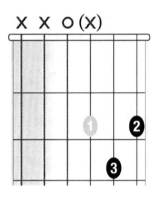

Boat Song

Duet No. 22

THE KEY OF A MINOR

The key of A minor is one of the most popular and easy to play keys on the guitar. Typical chords encountered in this key include its home chord A minor, as well as the E major and E[7]. Notice for A minor, there are no "x's, meaning that you may use all six strings when strumming.

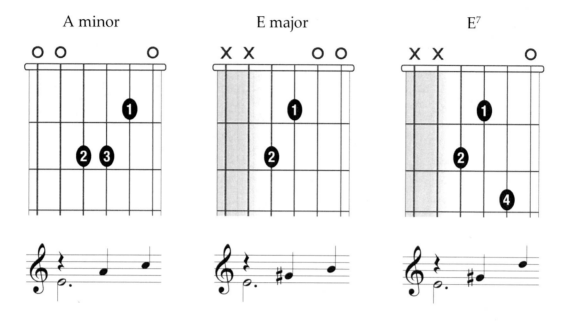

Practice strumming:

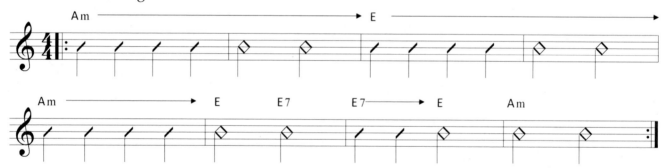

When you feel secure with the exercise above, proceed to *Etude Antique* in the key of A minor. Notice the piece begins with a smaller version of the A minor chord. Also, the 5th line presents two challenges: at m. 37 a finger exchange occurs where 2 on A (la) from the previous measures is exchanged for 3 on A (la); and at m. 38 there is a D♯ on ④.

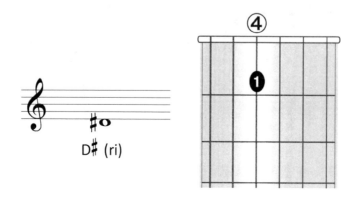

Etude Antique

Solo No. 15

M.M. ♩ = 150

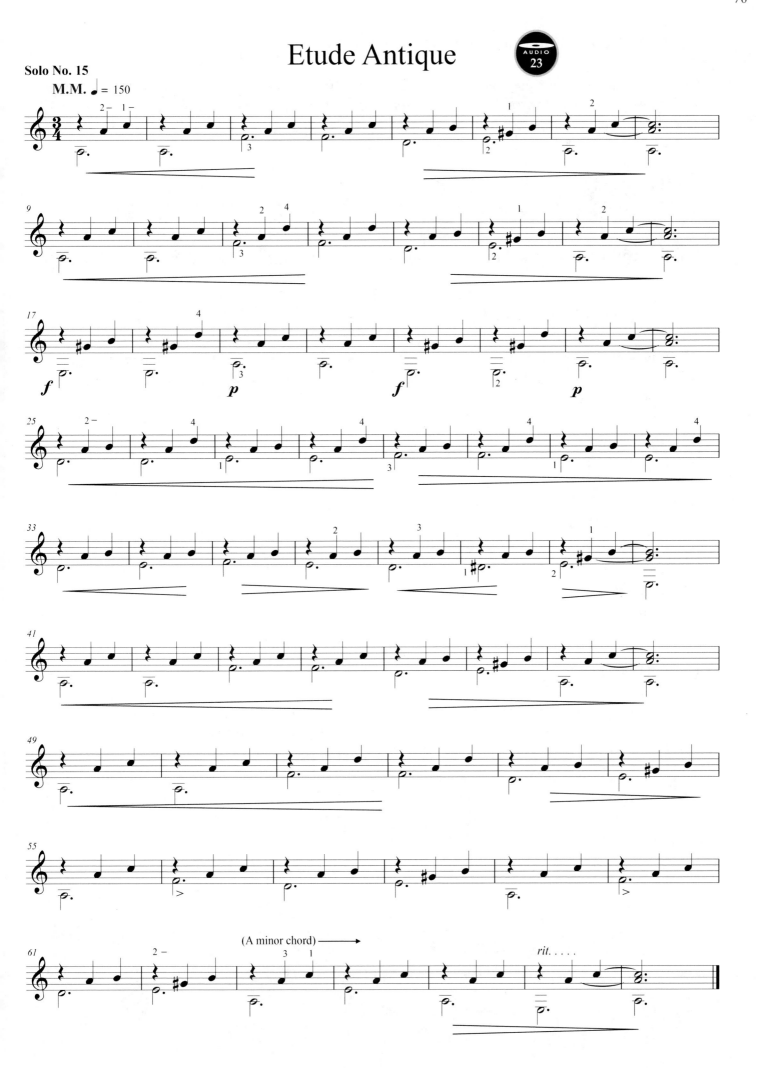

(A minor chord) ⟶

rit. . . . .

I-M-A FREE STROKE WITH CHORDS

Free stroke with *i-m-a* allows you now to play three notes of a chord simultaneously. To begin, anchor *p* on ⑤ to steady your hand. Place *i-m-a* on ④③② and solidly follow through with free stroke. You should concentrate on the firm placement and flexion of *a*. Practice on the open-string G chord:

The procedure for reading three notes is the same for reading dyads—read from bottom to top (see pp. 36-7).

ENHARMONIC NOTES

The following piece, *Simple Song VI* uses *i-m-a* free stroke on ④③②. The duet presents a few new concepts including the introduction of two flat notes, A♭ (le—pronounced *lay*) and E♭ (me—pronounced *may*):

A♭ (le)   E♭ (me)

You may notice that A♭ and E♭ are exactly where G♯ and D♯ are formed. When two differently spelled notes share the same pitch, they are said to be *enharmonic* with one another. Deciding on the appropriate note spelling is based on the key and harmonies of the piece[10].

GLIDE SHIFT

Simple Song VI also introduces a new left-hand challenge. Notice below, the 2nd finger on A moves down to G♯. When moving, keep the 2nd finger in contact with the string throughout. <u>Do not lift it from the string</u>. This is a technique called a *glide shift*.

Also from the C chord in m.13, the 2nd finger shifts down to E♭.

These fingerings will allow you to play more smoothly or legato.

---

[10] For more information on keys, see Aaron Shearer's *Supplement 2 Music Theory*, Alfred Publishing.

When pre-reading *Simple Song VI,* it may be helpful to block out the left hand by strumming each chord.

Simple Song VI

NEW 3-STRING CHORDS IN THE KEY OF A MINOR

Simple Song VII uses the same right-hand technique as *Simple Song VI*, but with *i-m-a* on the ③②① string group. Be sure to extend from the elbow to maintain the optimal hand position. The piece is in the key of A minor and Am and E chords figure prominently. In addition, there are several new chords including B♭ major and the B diminished, a quality indicated by the symbol: °.

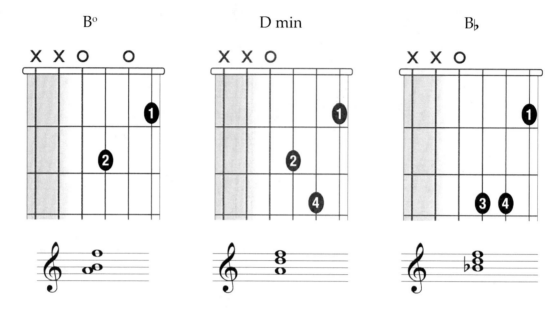

Practice strumming:

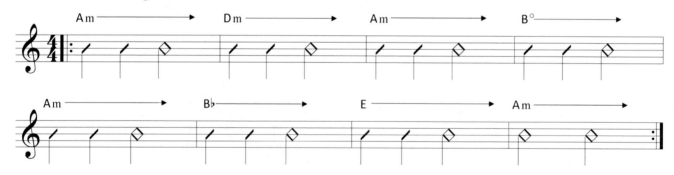

As with Simple Song VI, when pre-reading block out the left hand by strumming each chord, working one line at a time

Simple Song VII

Duet No. 24

CHORD COLORING

Very often a finger may be added or subtracted from a chord shape to slightly alter its sound. This is referred to as *chord coloring*. The letter name of the chord remains the same, but its quality slightly changes. Remember the quality is indicated by a suffix, such as *minor*, *sus4* or *7*. Review and play the following:

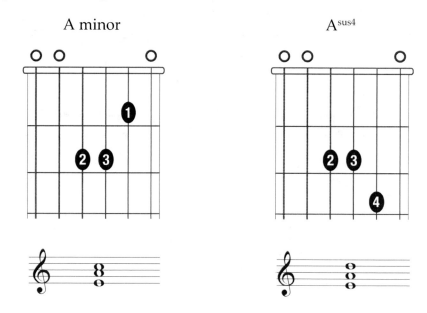

Notice that both patterns are a type of A chord. The lower notes remain the same; only the fingering on string ② differs. Re-fingering the D minor chord provides opportunity for similar coloring.

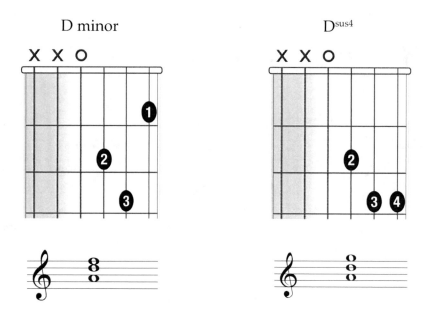

Again both patterns are a type of D chord. The lower notes remain the same; only the fingering on string ① is different.

With new chords comes greater challenge moving from one left-hand shape to the next. In particular, there may be difficulty placing the 4th finger to form both the A^{sus4} and D^{sus4} chord. As always, isolate and practice any new movement until it is coordinated. Slowly practice the following:

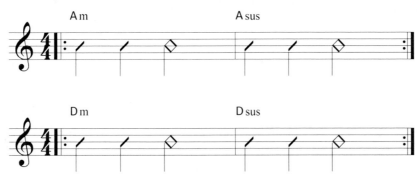

When you feel secure with the above, strum the following:

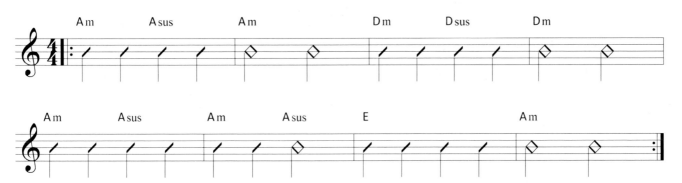

Before proceeding to the next duet, *Simple Song VIII*, be sure to securely visualize and learn the A and D chord forms above. The first measure of *Simple Song VIII* begins with this challenge of independence between the third and fourth finger. Be sure to visualize and learn this *movement form* securely before proceeding. When pre-reading, watch for measures where right-hand string crossings are needed. Remember string crossings are always executed from the elbow.

Simple Song VIII

Duet No. 25

INTRODUCING EIGHTH NOTES

DVD 45

The *eighth note* as its name implies, is half the duration of a quarter note. In learning to count and play eighth values, begin by establishing the quarter note pulse. Insert the word *"and"* in between each numbered count. This divides the beat into two equal halves: the number count is the strong half or *downbeat* and *"&"* is the weak half or *upbeat*.

Count and clap the following:

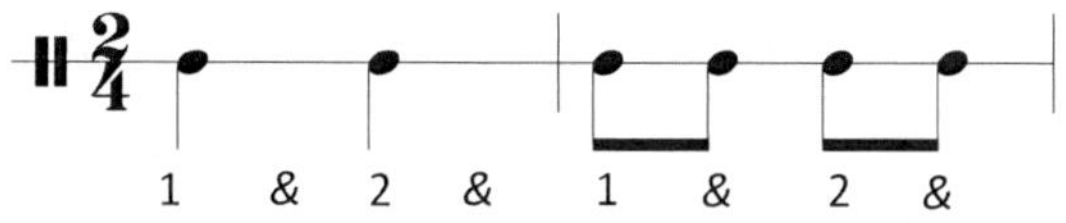

The eighth note is written two ways: a single eighth note has a "flag" attached to the side of its stem, or ; two or more eighth notes in succession, are often connected by a "beam": or or , . The *eighth rest* is likewise half the value of a quarter rest and is written: .

Ex. 22 presents eighth-note values for you to count and play. Begin by positioning your right hand to practice these rhythms on the back of your left hand with *p* extending and flexing in the usual manner (see the DVD). Practice as slowly as necessary until the motion is fluent. First repeat each measure, then practice straight through without repeating single measures. Aim for a steady rhythmic flow. If you feel insecure and must hesitate, go slower! Finally, these exercises should be practiced on each open string, ④, ⑤, and ⑥ with *i-m-a* resting on ① to stabilize the hand. The ultimate challenge is to be able to count aloud while playing.

Ex. 22a

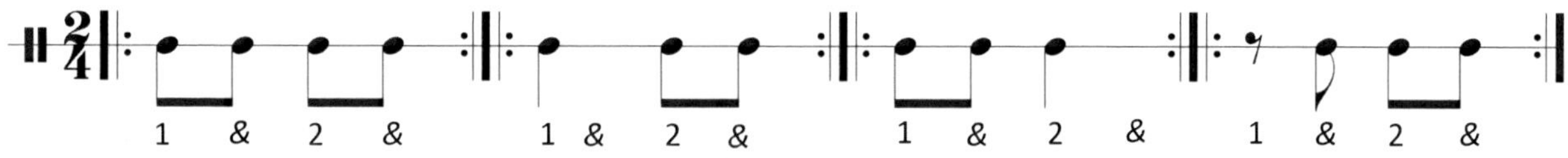

Ex. 22b

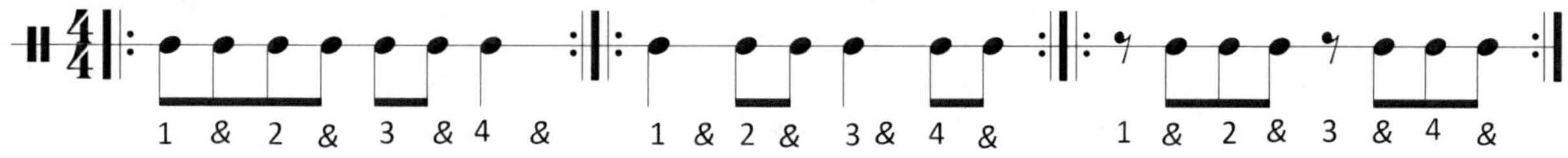

Ex. 22c

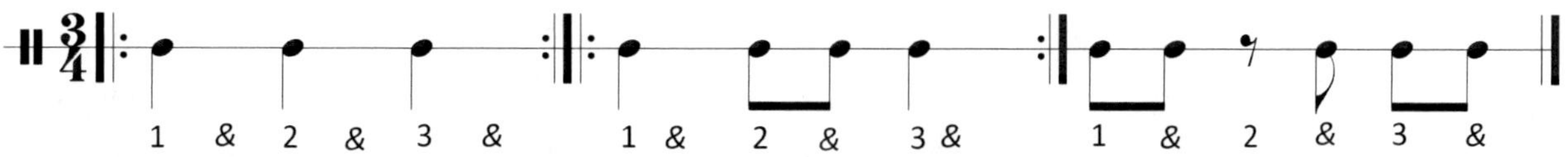

ALTERNATION OF *P* WITH *I-M-A*

The following set of pieces, starting with *Iberian Dance,* focus on the alternation of *p* and *i-m-a.* The first is rhythmically expressed with *p* on the downbeat and fingers on the upbeat. The execution is the same as alternating *p* and *i-m*; remember to prepare *i-m-a,* as *p* plays and prepare *p* as *i-m-a* play.

Ex. 23
Practice:

Iberian Dance Chords

Iberian Dance is in the key of A minor and uses the already familiar A minor, E major, and E⁷ chords. At m.10 and at the end of the piece, the E chord has been notated with a squiggly vertical line. This indicates to strum somewhat slowly across the strings. For the fullest sound, use the 6-string form of the chord:

E major

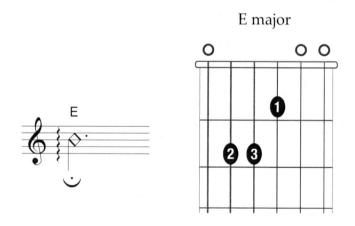

Iberian Dance

Solo No. 16

ALTERNATION OF *P* WITH *I-M-A* – SYNCOPATION

In the following solo *Lament*, notice that *i-m-a* chords are on strong downbeats, while *p* plays weak upbeats. At times, this situation gives rise to an interesting rhythmic pattern called *syncopation*. Syncopation occurs when *weak* beats are stressed with added duration.

To clearly understand syncopation, clap and count the following:

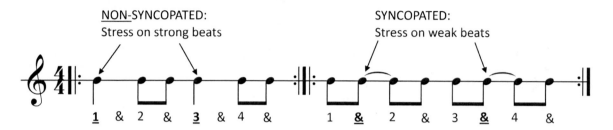

In the first measure, beats 1 and 3 are stressed with quarter-note durations. Since these are strong beats, they are not syncopated. In the second measure, the ties on the *& of 1* and *& of 3* add duration to weak beats. These are the syncopations.

In *Lament*, an example of syncopation occurs on the *& of 3* in the bass. Practice counting and playing the following:

THIS PAGE LEFT INTENTIONALLY BLANK

Lament

Solo No. 17

P, I, M, A ARPEGGIO

The next set of pieces, starting with *Russian Dance,* develops the *p, i, m, a* arpeggio. Prepare *i-m-a,* as *p* flexes; *m* moves sympathetically with *i* and *a* moves sympathetically with *m*; then prepare *p* as *a* flexes.

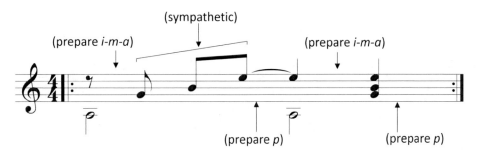

Russian Dance

Solo No. 18

92

COMMON-TONE FINGERINGS

Solo No. 19, *Dreaming,* is a *p,i,m,a* study played entirely on strings ④③②①. The main left-hand challenge involves changing chord shapes which are connected with *common-tone fingerings.* Study and strum the following 4-chord progression taken from the first two measures of *Dreaming*:

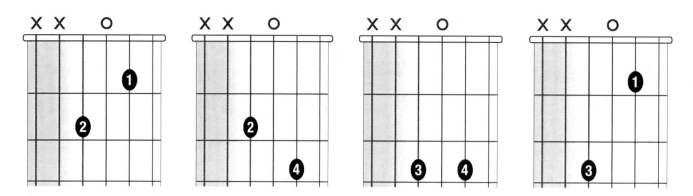

Common tone fingerings are shown below from measure to measure—first, **E** on ④ is the common-finger. Next, **D** on ② and, finally, **F** on ④ are common fingers. Being aware of these kinds of left-hand connections will visually aid and ultimately quicken your learning.

When pre-reading *Dreaming,* you'll encounter a rhythmic and technical challenge at mm. 25-6. To clarify, count aloud and tap out the rhythm on the guitar's soundboard:

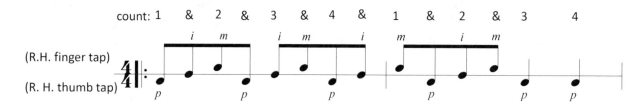

Dreaming

Solo No. 19

POSITION SHIFTING

The next solo, *Etude in A minor* requires the *p, i, m, a* arpeggio be played with continuity. Remember: as *a* moves sympathetically with *m* to sound its string, *p* extends and prepares for its next stroke.

In addition, there are a few left-hand challenges. Recall that B may be played on string ③ at fret IV. This B is necessary when notes on string ② are formed at the same time. Measure 2 of the following excerpt from *Etude in A minor* illustrates the need:

. . . . . which is realized in the following fingerboard patterns:

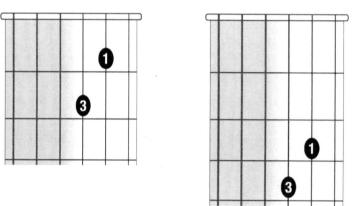

Furthermore to play this passage, a shift of two frets is in order. Since this distance takes your hand out of normal position, the movement is called a *position shift*. The entire left forearm must move along the neck, keeping the left-hand thumb centered behind the fingers. To accurately target this distance, practice shifting while looking at the fingerboard. Maintain your left-hand shape and focus on your 1st finger gliding from Frets I to III.

Etude in A minor

Solo No. 20

Beginning Free-Stroke Alternation on Adjacent Strings

 Free-stroke alternation of the fingers is one of the most challenging and rewarding movements you must develop in learning to play the classic guitar, allowing you to play accurately, powerfully, and rapidly. The importance of a fluent ability to alternate securely cannot be overstated. Consequently, it makes sense to take care in developing this ability clearly and patiently so that you can use it easily as your playing develops.

Alternation is the opposite of sympathetic movement. When moving sympathetically, the fingers move in the same direction; when alternating, they must move in opposite directions. Proceeding slowly and carefully, review the following procedure and the DVD to develop clear aims—you are laying the foundation for much of your future playing. Since in the optimal hand position *i* and *m* naturally fall on adjacent strings, and since your first experience with free stroke was in playing dyads, beginning alternation will occur on adjacent strings.

THE *P, I, M, I* ARPEGGIO

You will begin alternation with the *p, i, m, i* arpeggio. This arpeggio contains a single alternation.

- Begin by placing *p* on ④, *i* on ③, and *m* on ②.
- Play *p* then *i* with your usual clear, loud free stroke.
- As *m* plays, extend *i* to prepare on ③ again—*this is the alternation.*
- Follow through with *i* while preparing *p.*
- As *p* plays, prepare the fingers again.

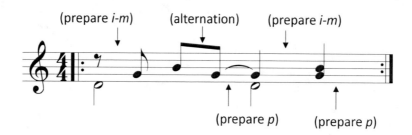

OPPOSED FINGER SWEEP EXERCISE

An important principle of alternation is the *flexion-extension relationship*—while a finger *flexes* to sound its string, another finger simultaneously *extends*, preparing to sound its string. This opposed motion of the fingers should be recognized as an unfamiliar movement in the scope of everyday activities. In view of this, fingers require special training which is carried out with the *Opposed Finger Sweep Exercise*. This drill is effective for acquiring the much needed independence and control for alternation.

- First place *p* against ⑥ to steady the hand.
- Keeping the hand stationary, proceed to sweep (lightly strum) the tips of *i* and *m* across the first three strings in opposed direction sweeping only on the flexion side.
- Be sure *a* and *c* are moving with *m* and that the fingers are moving from the middle and basal joints. The sweeps should be felt in precise, opposed motion.
- Do this gently at first, and rest briefly at the first feeling of forearm fatigue.

This is an effective exercise for acquiring independence and control for free stroke alternation. When through sufficient practice this exercise becomes fluent, begin sweeping across the three strings during flexion and extension simultaneously (see DVD 49).

In the following Solo No. 21 at m.10, there is a *natural sign* enclosed in parentheses (♮). The sign means the note is neither sharp nor flat and the parentheses make this a *courtesy accidental*. By rule, a courtesy accidental is not actually necessary but simply serves to remind that the note is natural. Courtesy accidentals are often used when a note has been affected by accidentals from a previous measure.

Pimi Etude in C *(preparatory)*

Solo No. 21

Pimi Etude in C

Solo No. 22

THE SIXTEENTH NOTE

Notes meant to sound rapidly are often written as *sixteenth notes*:

 Sixteenths are notated with two beams and receive half the value of eighth notes. There are 4 sixteenths in the time of a quarter note, counted: "**1**-*ee-&-ah*, **2**-*ee-&-ah*, etc." Subdivision of the quarter note is illustrated below. Notice the sixteenth rests (𝄿) on beats 3 and 4 of the third line.

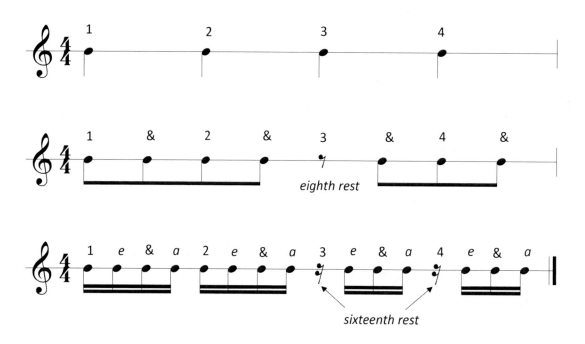

When sixteenths and eighths are combined, they are notated as follows:

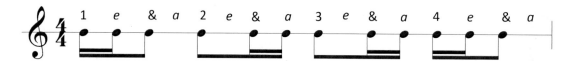

Following is a re-write of previous solo, *Solo No. 22* notated with sixteenth notes. Count and play:

THE DOTTED-QUARTER NOTE

Recall that a dot next to a note extends its duration by one half (p.29). Thus a dotted-quarter note equals the time of a quarter + an eighth.

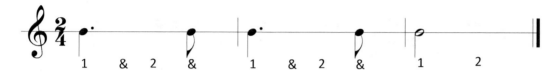

Count and clap the following:

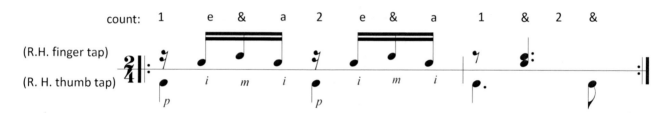

The following solo, *Meditation* makes use of both the sixteenth-and dotted-quarter values. To prepare the right hand, practice tapping the following rhythmic figures on the guitar's soundboard.

THE KEY OF E MINOR

Another very typical guitar key, *E minor*, is the setting of the following solo *Meditation*. Its home note (starting and ending note) is E and its key signature has one sharp—F♯, meaning that all F's are now F♯.

This includes *F♯ on* ① and new note: *F♯ on* ④ played with 4 at fret IV.

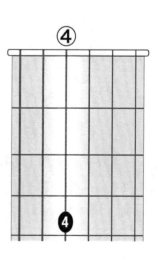

Meditation

Solo No. 23

Chords for *Moonlight*

The following solo, *Moonlight,* is in the key of D major. In addition to including the already familiar D and A major chords, several new 4-string chords are introduced:

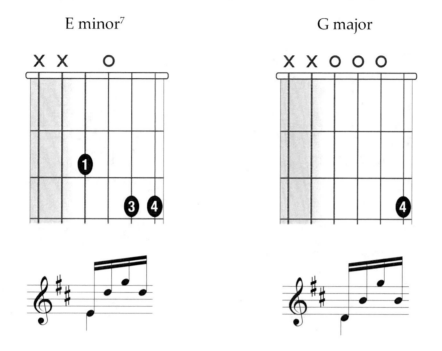

Practice strumming the following progression of chords:

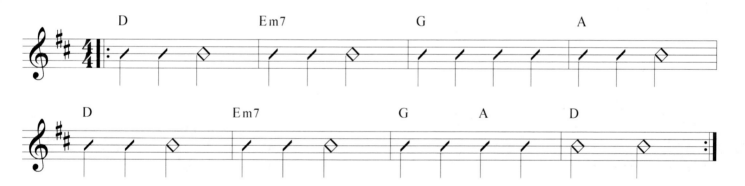

Other new chord patterns include the B minor and the A♯°(diminished) chord which includes an A♯ on ③ at III:

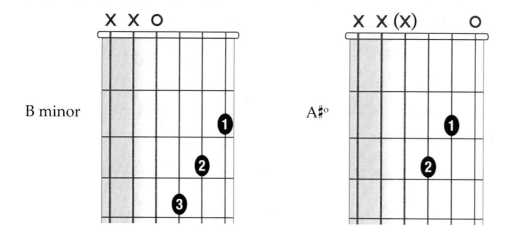

B minor   A♯°

Practice strumming:

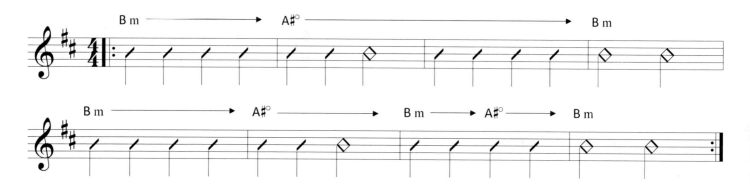

HARMONICS ON THE VII FRET

Thus far, you've played harmonics only at fret XII. In *Moonlight,* you'll find harmonics at VII which sound five notes higher than those at XII. This can be confusing because while notated as open strings, harmonics at VII do not match written pitches. For example, *Moonlight* is in the key of D and has a home chord of D major. Yet its final chord (m. 44) appears to be G major, with notes G and B. However, marked as VII harmonics, the notes actually sound D and F♯ of the D chord.

Sounding harmonics at VII requires a little more skill than XII. The touch spot, or *node* as it's called, is somewhat narrower and can be trickier to locate. Touch with 3:

THIS PAGE LEFT INTENTIONALLY BLANK

Moonlight

Solo. No. 24

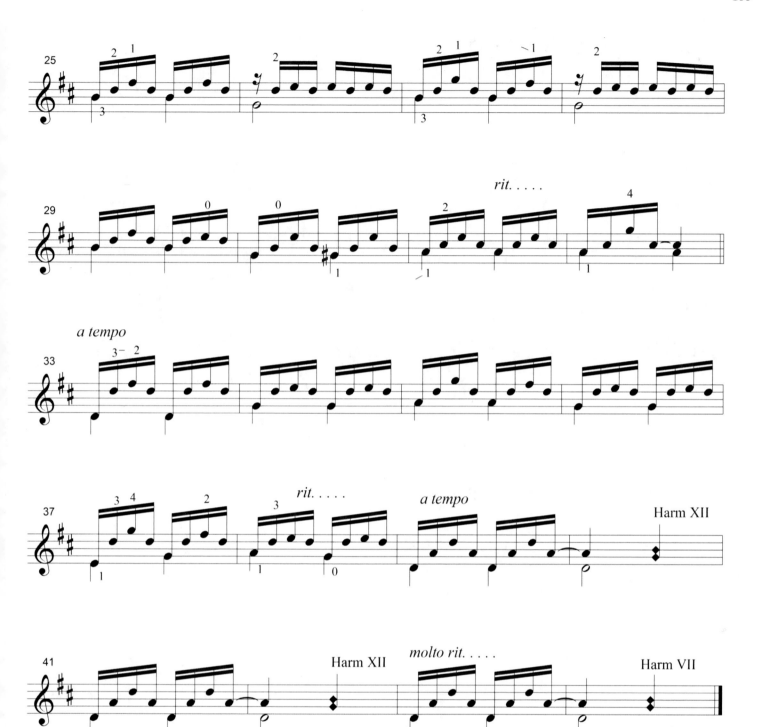

NOTES ON STRINGS ⑤

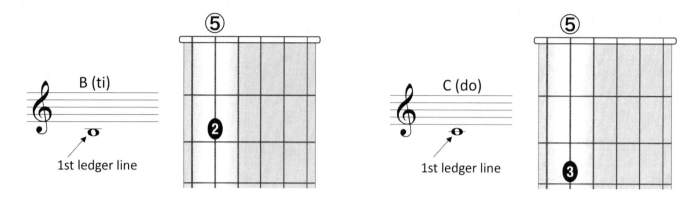

Ex.24

NOTES ON STRINGS ⑥

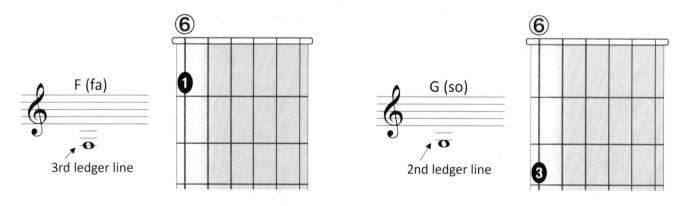

Ex. 25a

Ex. 25b

Remember to pre-read, vocalize and air-guitar.

Simple Song IX

Duet No. 26

The Key of E minor—six strings

Remember that the key of E minor has one sharp—F♯—which affects all registers including F♯ on ①, F♯ on ④, and F♯ on ⑥. The low F♯ on ⑥ is diagrammed to the right.

When playing an E minor piece involving 6 strings, you must clearly visualize all accidentals (on the fingerboard) which are part of its musical environment. The following solos, *Waltz in E minor* and *Etude in E minor*, offer this challenge.

A Higher Fingerboard Position

Observe the fingering in the following bass line from Solo No. 25.

Notice the G can easily be played as string ③. However, 4 is available to form it at fret V of ④, which requires slightly shifting your left-hand position. This option allows G to sound with expressive warmth, which would not otherwise be possible as an open string.

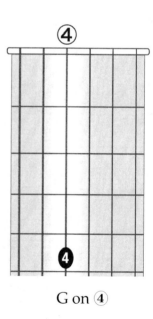

G on ④

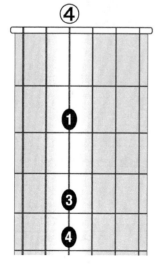

Practice playing G on ④ in this higher fingerboard position:

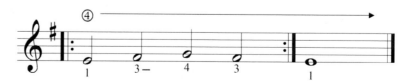

Waltz in E minor

Solo No. 25

Etude in E minor

Solo No. 26

G minor Blues

The following solo, *G minor Blues* offers several new challenges. First, the piece may be played in swing rhythm, which is a performance style typical of jazz or blues. Swing rhythm is produced by interpreting evenly notated eighth notes as a lilting long-short pattern. To execute, think of each beat as having three parts—**1**-*&-a*, **2**-*&-a*, etc. with the first eighth on the number and the second eighth on the "a." Count and clap the following swing rhythm:

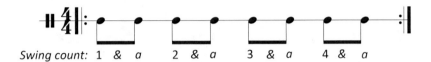

The swing count may be applied to the right-hand pattern (open strings) of the first measure of *G minor Blues:*

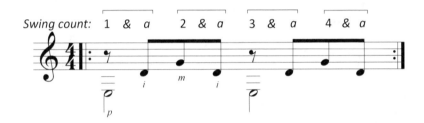

In addition there is a courtesy accidental at m.14 and a new note: B♭(te) on ⑤ introduced at m. 14.

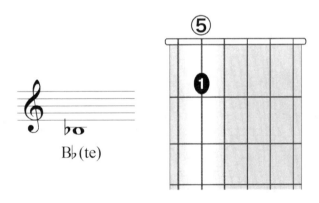

B♭(te)

G minor Blues

Solo No. 27

(**To the Teacher:** eighth notes
may be played in swing rhythm)

$\frac{3}{8}$ TIME

In notating music that moves at a relatively fast tempo, composers often use the meter, $\frac{3}{8}$ meaning the time of three ♪'s in each measure. In this meter the numbered count (*1, 2, 3*) falls on the eighth; the *&* falls on the sixteenth.

An entire measure of $\frac{3}{8}$ would be notated with the dotted-quarter note (♩.). Practice counting and clapping the following:

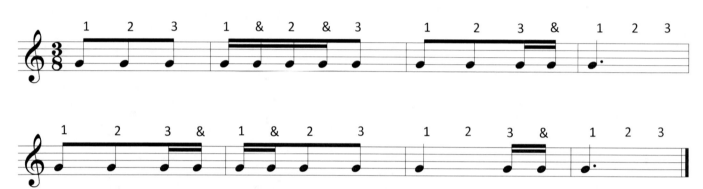

Soaring

Solo No. 28

COMPOUND METER

All the meters you've encountered so far (2/4, 3/4, 4/4, 4/8, etc) are called *simple meters*. A simple meter is where the beat naturally subdivides into two equal parts and can be counted: **1-&, 2-&**, etc.

Compound meter differs in that a dotted value (♩.) represents the beat and that each beat subdivides into three equal parts. Compound meters are classified by the number of dotted values present in each measure.

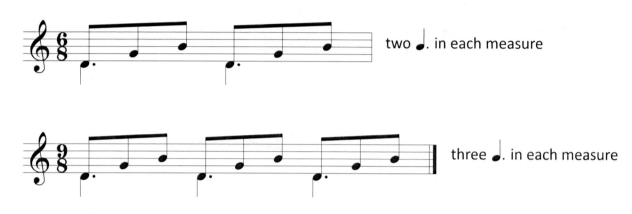

two ♩. in each measure

three ♩. in each measure

Since **6/8** has two ♩. beats, it's referred to as compound *duple* meter. Technically it is counted:

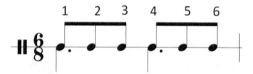

But this manner of counting doesn't truly express the accent pattern of the measure. A more effective way to feel compound duple is to count in groups of three's: **1-&-a, 2-&-a** as in swing rhythm.

Practice this method of counting in the following example. Count aloud while clapping the rhythms, making sure to accentuate the groupings of three.

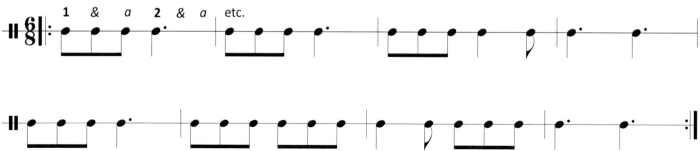

Following are typical examples of compound duple meter with the melody in the bass.
Practice counting and playing:

Three Compound Meter Studies

Study 3

UNDERSTANDING CHORDS

Your earliest chords involved patterns of three strings (as in *Etude in C*). Actually these patterns are part of larger 4-, 5- and 6-string chords on the guitar. To understand why, consider how chords are constructed on the staff.

We begin by recognizing that only *three* tones are needed to build a chord. On the staff this appears as every other note, with the lowest note naming the chord. This naming note is called the *root*. Thus, to build a C chord, we would need C, E, and G.

The other parts of the chord are called the 3rd (3 notes above the *root*) and the 5th (5 notes above the *root*). In the diagram below, E is the 3rd and G is the 5th.

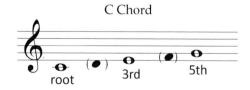

These three parts —*root, 3rd* and *5th*— define and spell the chord, just like specific combinations of letters spell a word. As we duplicate chord parts higher or lower, their names remain the same. In other words, any C in a C chord is understood as the *root*; any E is a *3rd* ; and any G is a *5th*.

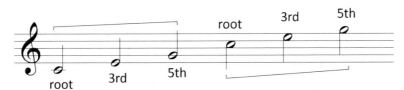

Once, the *root, 3rd* and *5th* are determined, the chord can be voiced in a number of ways on the guitar. For example, a 3-string C chord can be easily formed with the *3rd* (E) as the bass and the *root* (C) on top.

A 4-string C chord with a doubled root can be voiced as:

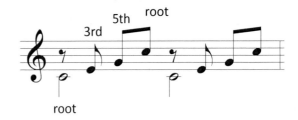

Its fingerboard pattern would appear as shown to the right.

Since the open strings ⑥ and ① may be included as chord tones (the *3rd*), this pattern is also suitable to strum as a 6-string chord.

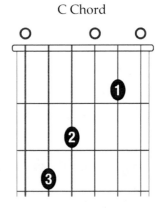

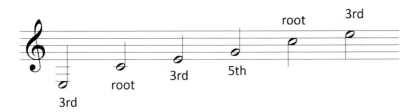

The next solo, *Peace*, uses the C chord above as well as several other chord patterns. As always, strings marked with an (x) indicate that you may include them in the strum, though they are not chord tones.

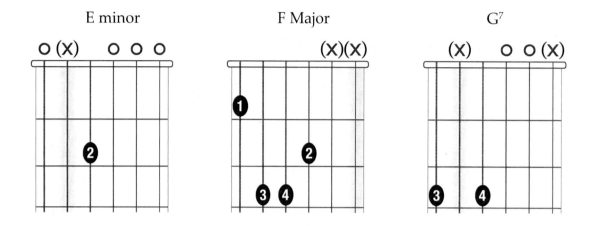

Strum the following exercise. Be sure to carefully visualize the chord shape as well as the movement needed to move from chord to another before proceeding. Notice the common 4th finger when moving between F and G⁷.

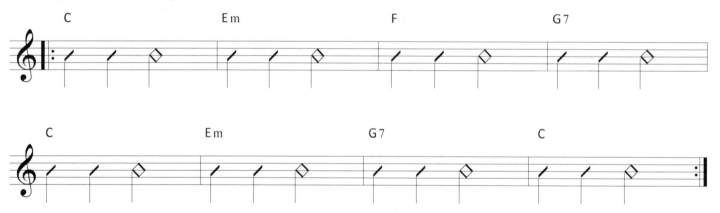

P, M, I ARPEGGIO

Peace is written in $\frac{6}{8}$ and is the first instance of the *p,m,i* arpeggio. The right-hand execution is very similar to the *p,i,m* pattern; the sympathetic motion now leads with *m*.

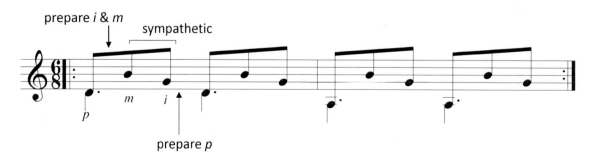

Peace

Solo No. 29

ALTERNATING WITH *A*

The next set of pieces will help to develop the alternation of *a*. You'll begin with the *p, i, m-a, i,* arpeggio; *m* & *a* move together followed by an alternation with *i*.

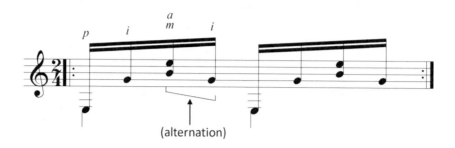

(alternation)

Duet No 27, *Country Road*, introduces several new chord shapes. The key is D, starting and ending with the familiar D chord. Beginning at m. 17, new chords are introduced, including a 6-string A major chord:

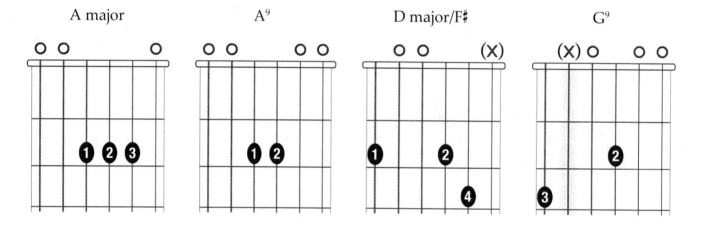

We can understand the A⁹ and G⁹ as colorings of the A and G major chords. Notice also there is a common tone for all four shapes—2 on A. Visualizing this while strumming will help you connect the movement forms.

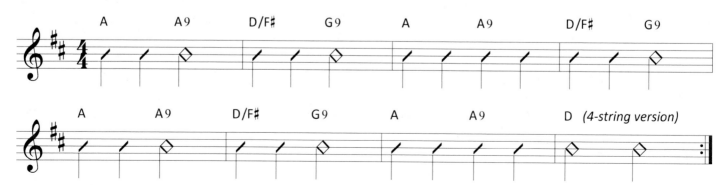

THIS PAGE LEFT INTENTIONALLY BLANK

THIS PAGE LEFT INTENTIONALLY BLANK

Country Road

Duet No. 27

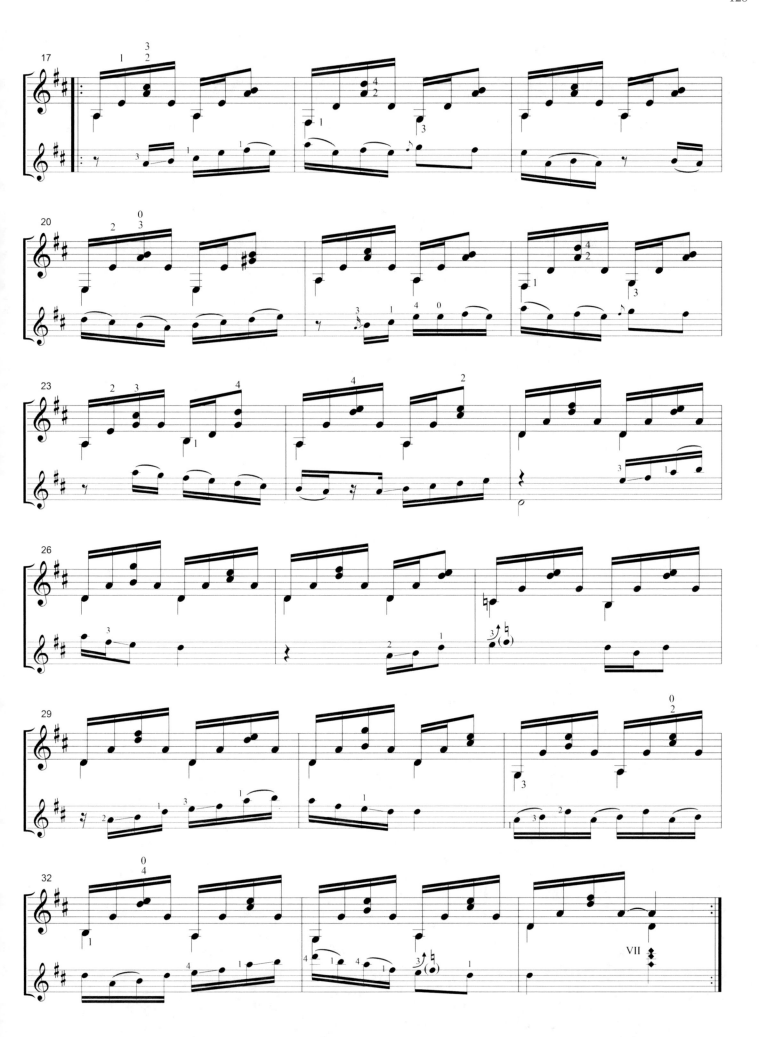

P, I, A ARPEGGIO

In the following pieces you will encounter the *p, i, a* arpeggio, and the related movement forms *p, i, a, i* and *p, i, a, i, a, i*. There is often a tendency for *m* to remain rigidly extended during these movement, which impedes the free movement of *i* and *a*. To correct this problem, continue to move *m* with *a*. For each piece practice the arpeggio on open strings using prepared stroke until you can execute them with reasonable security.

Serenade

Solo No. 30

Ancient Voices

Solo No. 31

Pastoral

Solo No. 32

133

Pastoral II

Solo No. 33

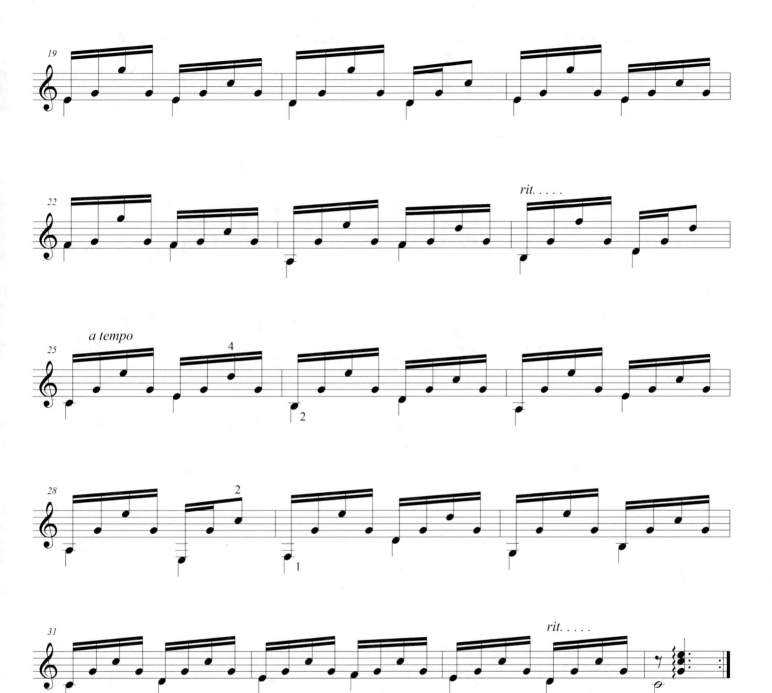

A minor Etude

Solo No. 34

M.M. ♪ = 115

PLAYING SINGLE NOTE FREE STROKES

So far every effort has been made to present curriculum that promotes the optimal hand position and sympathetic motion, minimizing any challenges that would hinder you from reinforcing these principles. By now your habits have been well reinforced and you are now ready to begin a new movement form; playing single notes with the fingers in free stroke. Begin playing single notes as follows:

- Prepare *p* on ③ to steady the hand, then prepare *m* on ① with *i* slightly flexed so that it no longer prepares on ②, leaving only *m* on ①.

- Flex *m* to sound ①, allowing the inactive fingers (including *i*) to follow through with *m*.

- Maintain the optimal hand position and notice how the inactive fingers move sympathetically with *m*.

- Next, prepare only *i* on ②, with *m* slightly flexed so that it is no longer prepared. Sound ② with *i* and allow *m* to move with the inactive fingers.

- Return to playing dyads (E and B String) frequently to ensure that you are maintaining the Optimal Hand Position for free stroke.

- Be sure you're using prepared stroke to develop a clear and powerful stroke.

- Play Ex. 26 using this procedure. Notice the dyads in mm. 3 & 6.

Ex. 26

- As you feel secure with *i* and *m* in single finger free stroke, flex from the elbow (string cross upward) and place *p* on ④ and *a* on ①. Have *i* and *m* slightly flexed so that they are no longer prepared. Sound ① with *a* and allow *i* and *m* to move with *a*.

- Play Ex. 27 using this procedure. Notice the dyads in mm. 3 & 6.

Ex. 27

CORRECTING THE OBJECTIONABLE SIDE-PULL

During individual free stroke, the *i* finger may tend to pull out of alignment to the left while the *a* and *m* fingers may tend to pull to the right. Unless corrected early on, this problem can become a habit, impeding free movement of the finger. The correction can effectively be approached through a simple "back-of-the-left-hand" exercise, similar to that introduced on p.48 and proceeding as follows and shown in the DVD:

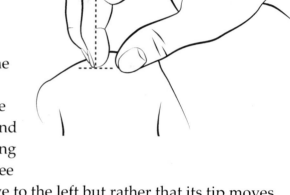

- Support the R.H. by placing the tip of *p* against the back of the L.H.

- Keep the middle joints of inactive fingers slightly flexed and the basal joints of all the fingers positioned in their comfortable midrange.

- Place the tip of *i* lightly against the back of the L.H. with the middle joint perpendicular to the point of tip contact with the back of the hand. Proceed to briefly prepare the stroke and then sharply flex the middle joint of *i*, touching only a small area of the hand to simulate a free stroke. Be sure that the finger does not swerve to the left but rather that its tip moves directly toward the middle joint of *p*.

When the simulated free-stroke movement feels secure and comfortable with *i*, position the right hand to practice sounding the open ③ with *i*, free stroke as follows:

- To simulate a free-stroke movement, position the middle joint of *i* over the open ③ and place *p* on a lower string (either ④ or ⑤) to support the hand. Practice sounding ③ free stroke using a slight "preparation" with *i* until secure.

When *i* feels secure, carry out the preceding routine with *m* on ② on and then *a* on ① while closely checking for direct, well-aligned flexion of each finger (a mirror is often helpful).

- Then practice Ex. 28, with *i, m* and *a.* with *p* placed on ④.

- Carefully maintain the optimal hand position along with a consistent free-stroke movement with each finger throughout the exercise.

Ex. 28

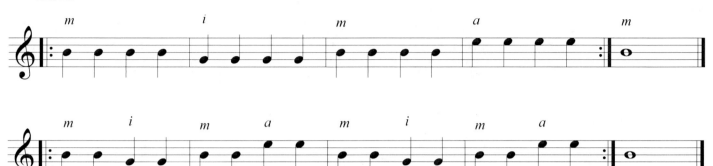

To train the fingers well and most quickly requires patience. You need to take time to thoughtfully carry out the prep-play procedure shown in Ex. 26 and explained in DVD 55.

SOUNDING NOTES WITH *P* AND A SINGLE FINGER FREE STROKE

Playing *p* and a single finger together can often be a challenging movement. When only a single finger is involved, the inactive fingers tend to become somewhat rigidly extended—impeding the movement of the active finger. Thus it's important to give special attention to the inactive fingers, ensuring that they remain slightly flexed and move with the active finger.

Begin with *p* and *m* sounding ⑤ and ① (free stroke), observing the following reminders:

- For security and best tone, begin with prepared stroke.
- Emphasize middle-joint movement and follow-through of the fingers.
- *P* should follow through freely, coming to rest against *i*.
- Keep inactive fingers slightly flexed and moving with *m*.
- During alternation of *p* and the fingers, as in m.2, be sure to prep *p* when the finger sounds and prep the finger when *p* sounds.
- Be sure to study the DVD to form clear aims for this movement.

When this movement feels secure, practice Ex. 29, first with *p-m*, then with *p-i*, then *p-a*. Notice that rests have been strategically placed to allow you to prepare your fingers and/or thumb.

Ex. 29

Up and Down

Solo No. 35

THIS PAGE LEFT INTENTIONALLY BLANK

Tanawha

Duet No. 28

Repertoire from the Masters

The past few centuries have provided the guitar with notable composers who were among the greatest guitarists of their time. That their music still regularly appears in new recordings and concerts all over the world is a testament to the excellence of their music. Each dedicated himself to the task of improving the technique of playing the guitar and establishing a better system of teaching it. Their written method books, while incomplete in the light of present day technique, are still valuable contributions to the literature for study of the guitar. Each of these masters helped to elevate the instrument to its present respected position in the world of music.

Along with their methods, these men wrote an unquestionably rich treasure of studies and concert compositions. Each wrote a tremendous amount of music ranging from easy etudes to pieces requiring enormous virtuosity. While the following selections belong to the former, each is a complete musical composition in itself. Some are tuneful with harmonic support, while others are arpeggio studies requiring fast and even execution with both hands for proper interpretation. The first section of these pieces is relatively short, but there will be others as you continue through the method and your technical proficiency increases.

Proper study of these works will be most helpful in your musical and technical development. Students may be assured that by carefully learning to play each composition they will better equip themselves for progress to larger works of even richer musical content.

You should memorize[11] the pieces presented here you find most appealing and add them to the repertoire of pieces you play for anyone interested in listening. Enjoy this rich heritage of the guitar.

---

[11] See *Book 2 Classic Guitar Developments* for complete information on memorization.

Estudio

D. Aguado

Allegro

F. Carulli

Op.14, No. 1

M Carcassi

Allegretto
Op. 44 No. 2

Fernando Sor

* Notice measures 7 & 8 contain free-stroke alternations on a single string - see p. 147 for a complete explanation.

Alternation

FREE-STROKE ALTERNATION ON A SINGLE STRING

At this point, alternation of *i* and *m* on <u>adjacent</u> strings should feel comfortable and secure. In the optimal hand position the shorter *i* is on the lower string and the longer *m* is on the higher string. When alternating *i* and *m* on a <u>single</u> string, the hand needs a slight adjustment—*m* plays slightly more flexed to accommodate the shorter *i* on the same string.

Experiment with this movement to find the position for the R.H. that feels most comfortable; try to achieve the following:

- Each finger should be able to execute a fluent and powerful free stroke, with no tendency to accidentally bump adjacent strings.
- Firmly follow through—do not allow a "lifting" of the fingers in order to clear the other strings.
- Carefully study the DVD to form clear aims.

Begin the following Solo No. 36 by using prepared stroke, to develop habits of precise placement of the fingers.

Single String Alternation I

Solo No. 36

D.C. al Coda

Sometimes music is written to have a special ending called a *coda* (meaning *tail* in Italian). In the following solo, *Single String Alternation Etude II*, notice the *D.C. al Coda* marking over the next-to-the-last measure. *D.C.* means to repeat back to the beginning; *al Coda*, means to play to the first ⊕ sign (end of m.15), and then jump to the coda marked by the second ⊕ sign (m. 33).

Single String Alternation II

Solo No. 37

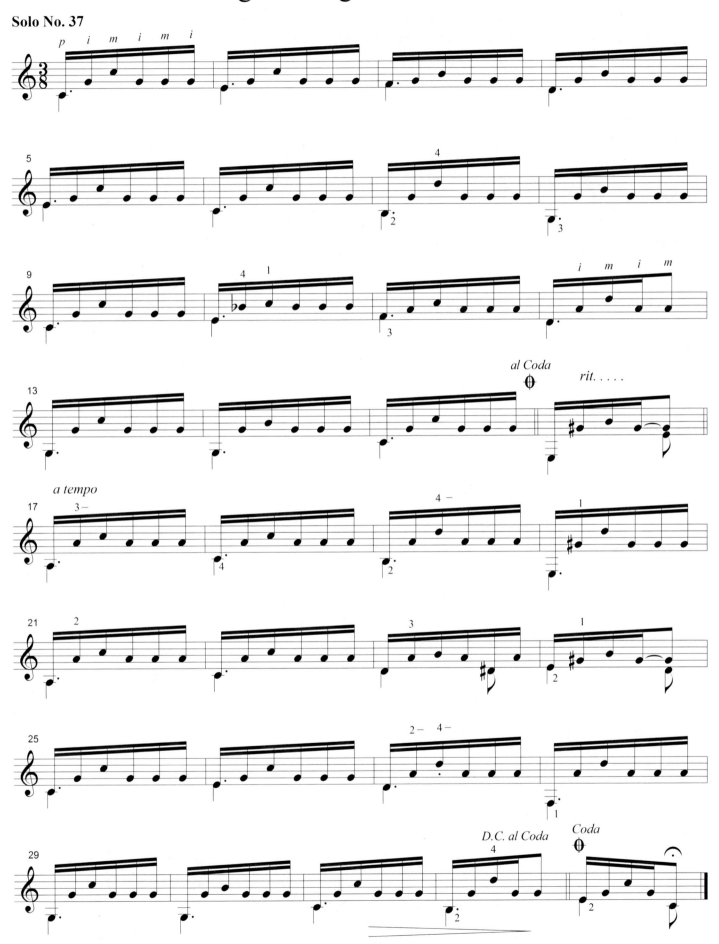

PRINCIPLES OF STRING CROSSING IN ALTERNATION

String crossing is the technique of shifting your right hand to maintain the optimal position of your fingers for sounding different strings. During *i* and *m* alternation, for example, *i* should always maintain a sufficiently flexed position at its middle joint to achieve maximum leverage—*m* will function in a slightly more flexed position. Therefore, when you begin to alternate on an adjacent string, you must shift your hand across the strings to maintain the optimal position of *i*. Secure string crossing is essential for executing rapid and accurate scales. In fact, a lack of speed or fluency in playing scales can often be traced to faulty string-crossing technique.

The best way to maintain the optimal hand position as you cross strings is to execute the crossing through movement from the elbow. This allows you to maintain good alignment in the R.H. without causing shoulder tension (see the DVD).

Begin with *i* on ⑥ at the upper area of the soundhole.

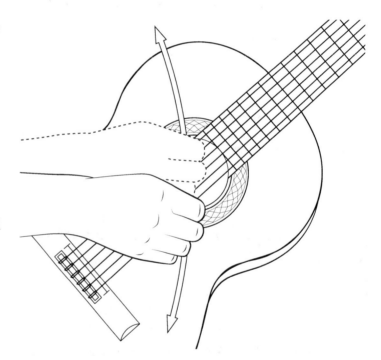

- <u>Slowly</u> play *i, m, i, m.*
- Shift to ① at the lower area of the soundhole and pause. Find the optimal hand position.
- <u>Slowly</u> play *i, m, i, m.*
- Shift to ⑥ at the upper area of the guitar's soundhole and pause. Find the optimal hand position.
- Repeat the procedure until secure.

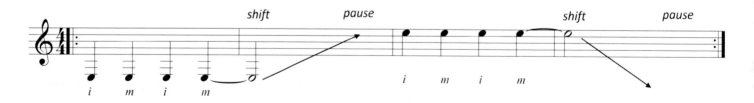

When shifting, make sure that you:

- Maintain good alignment of the wrist while crossing.
- Keep the tilt of the hand consistent while crossing; do not allow the arm to rotate as you move.

Next, follow the procedure above but shift one string across and back:

Ex. 30

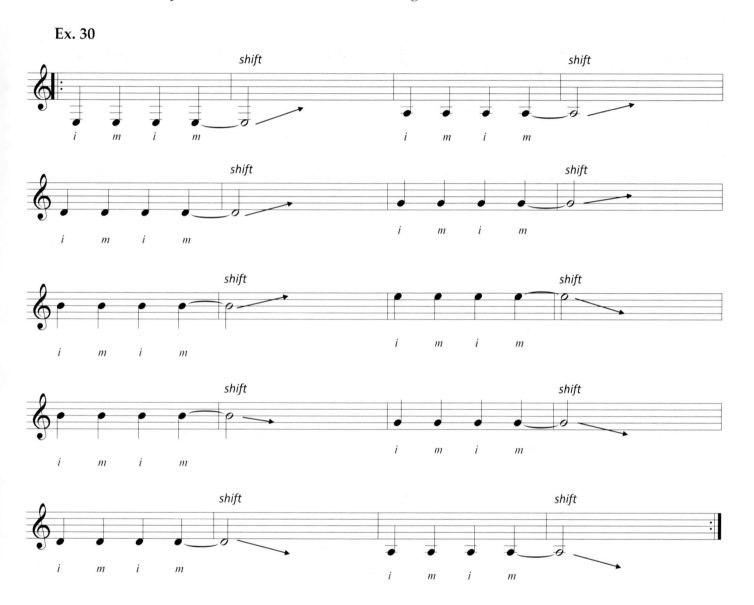

String crossing is applied in the following set of five Etudes. In the beginning, string crossing movement is slight while gradually increasing with each Etude.

String Crossing Etude I

Solo No. 38

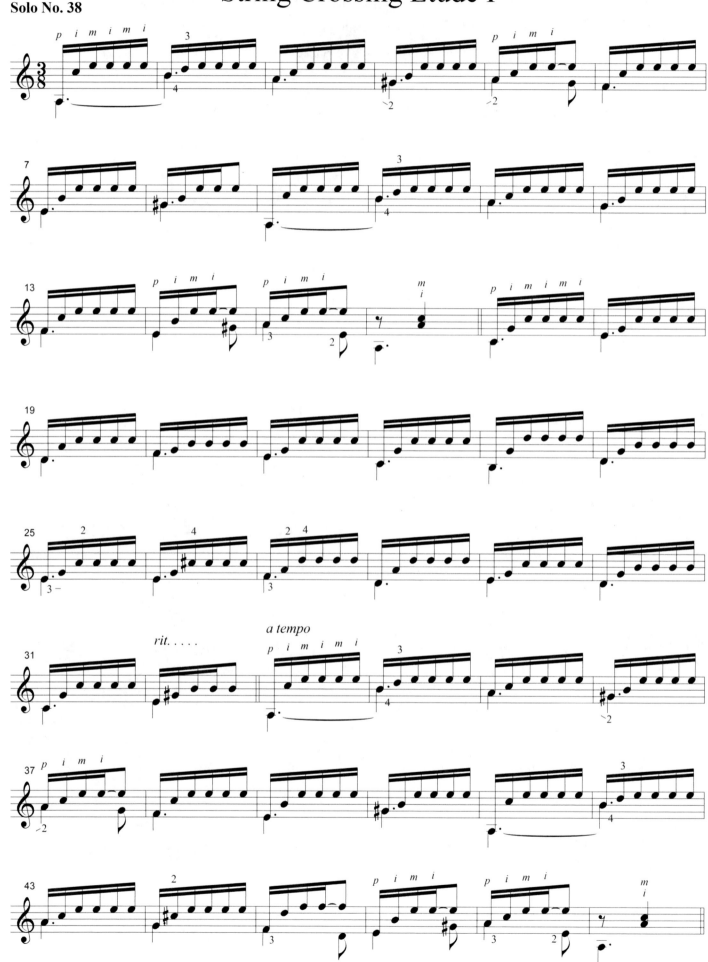

String Crossing Etude II

Solo No. 39

String Crossing Etude III

Solo No. 40

THIS PAGE LEFT INTENTIONALLY BLANK

ALTERNATE FINGERINGS FOR CHALLENGING STRING CROSSINGS – CROSS FINGERINGS

In the previous etudes, *m* has led in crossing to the higher string, and *i* has led in crossing to the lower string. Because of the differing reaches of *i* and *m*, this procedure feels more secure in beginning string crossing. But, in playing certain musical passages, it's not always practical to lead to the higher string with *m* or a lower string with *i*. This situation is called a *cross fingering*.

Solos No. 41 and 42 present a challenge which may be resolved by using two different right-hand fingerings. Begin by learning the fingering not shown in parenthesis. When secure, re-learn the piece using the alternate fingering shown in parenthesis.

- The fingering in the example below requires a cross fingering—a reverse order where *i* leads to the higher string and *m* leads to the lower string (indicated by arrows). This is no doubt challenging and should be practiced as another facet of right-hand training.

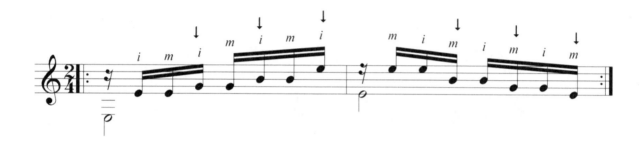

- The fingering in this next example resolves the cross fingering by incorporating three fingers, allowing *a* to reach to the higher string. This eases the string crossing problem but requires greater control of *a* which now alternates with *m*.

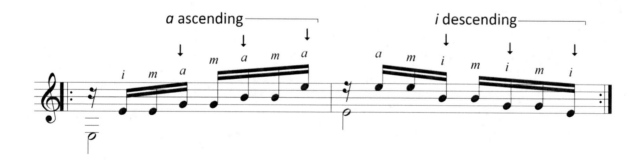

As a rule cross fingerings should be minimized by substituting the *a* finger but in reality this cannot always be avoided especially in scale passages.

String Crossing Etude IV

Solo No. 41

String Crossing Etude V

Solo No. 42

P, I, M, A, M, I ARPEGGIO

The *p, i, m, a, m, i* arpeggio is made of a combination of two sympathetic and one opposed movements. Proceed as follows:

- Begin by preparing *p* on ④ with *ima* on ③, ② and ①.
- After *p* plays, allow *i, m, a* to move sympathetically across their strings.
- As *a* plays, prepare *i, m* on ③ and ②. This is the opposed movement. Free stroke *m* and *i* sympathetically across their strings.
- As *i* plays, prepare *p*.
- As *p* plays, again allow *i-m-a* to reset on ③, ②, ① and the pattern repeats.

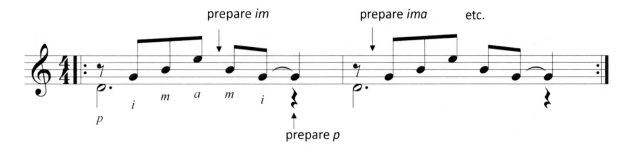

When you feel secure with the above exercise, practice *p, i, m, a, m, i* with continuity. Remember to follow the same procedures above, preparing at the same points and feeling the appropriate sympathetic and opposed movements. Practice without rhythmic pause:

Traveler

Solo No. 43

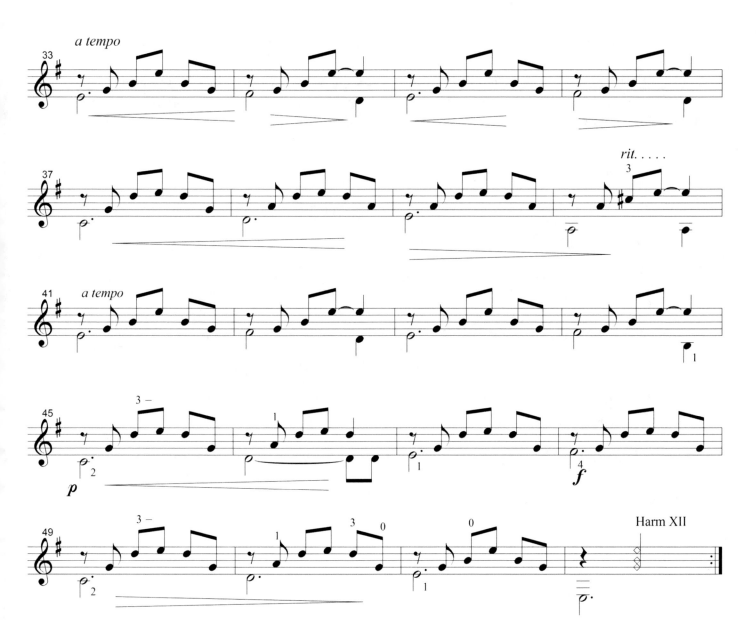

163

ONE ARPEGGIO — TWO DIFFERENT METERS

The 6 strokes of the *p, i, m, a, m, i* arpeggio can be organized into two different rhythmic patterns or meters— *three groups of two* or *two groups of three*. The technical execution of the arpeggio—*preparation, sympathetic motion,* and *alternation*— remains the same, though stressing different fingers changes the accent pattern. Stressing *m*, produces **3/4** (simple meter) and stressing *a*, gives **6/8** (compound meter).

Experience the difference in the following:

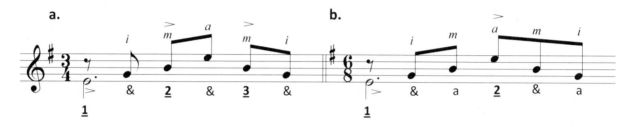

Notice that both measures **a.** & **b.** are identical except for meter and manner of counting. *Traveler*, your last piece, was written in **3/4** ; your next solo, *Tristement* is in **6/8** .

When pre-reading, be sensitive to this shift to counting compound meter.

Tristement also introduces the note C♯ on ⑤ at IV:

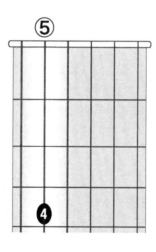

THIS PAGE LEFT INTENTIONALLY BLANK

Tristement

Solo No. 44

THE PICK-UP

The following duet No. 29 starts with a *pick-up* measure. This is an incomplete measure with only a single beat. In $\frac{3}{4}$ this is counted as the 3rd beat. To start the piece, prepare by counting 1, 2….. the teacher's part begins on the 3rd (pick-up) beat.

Si Bheag Si Mhor

Duet No. 29

trad. Celtic

PLAYING SCALES

A *scale* is a consecutive series of step notes. Our first scale includes all of the natural notes (no sharps or flats) on the guitar, and begins and ends on the guitar's lowest note, E. Since the scale includes all *open strings*, it is referred to as the *open- position scale*. To focus more fully on training your right hand you should first visualize and memorize the open-position scale. Proceed as follows:

- Beginning with low E ⑥, read and say the solfege syllable and finger number for each note as follows: *mi-0* ("oh" for open), *fa-1, so-3, la-0,* etc.

- Air-guitar, maintaining steady rhythm. Clearly visualize each finger and each string/fret as though you're actually playing the notes.

- When secure, carry out the procedure from memory until you can maintain a flowing pace without hesitations. Then take the guitar and prepare to play.

- Slowly and carefully play the scale, using *i* and *m* alternation. Continue to solfege each note. Also, clearly visualize and feel the placement of each left-hand finger.

- Establish a feeling of precise alternation and string crossing. Emphasize accurate rhythms and evenness of volume between tones. When secure, accelerate the tempo, but continue to play without hesitation.

Ex. 31

You may also practice the open-position scale alternating with *m* & *i*, *a* & *m*, or *m* & *a*.
Next practice playing the open-position scale with 2 strokes per note:

Ex. 32

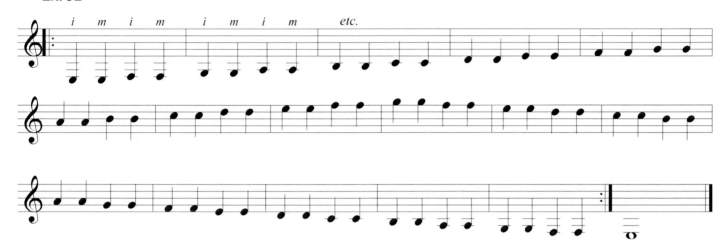

1 stroke per note

When you shifted from string to string in the above exercise, the start finger was always the same. Scales with 1 stroke per note pose a new challenge. Due to the nature of the guitar's tuning, string crossing involves shifting to adjacent strings with a different start finger. Practice the following exercise on open strings to develop this ability, carefully watching the hand and maintaining a consistently firm stroke in sounding each string:

Ex. 33

Adding the left hand to the above pattern of alternation and string crossing produces the scale with one stroke per note. Practice slowly at first, gradually increasing the tempo when secure.

Ex. 34

Ex. 35 is a reading exercise. First scan the exercise to determine its general shape and design. Solfege and visualize before playing, isolating any challenging movement forms; then practice slowly and accurately. Gradually increase the tempo as you become secure with alternation, string crossing, and tone production.

Ex. 35

OPEN-POSITION C MAJOR SCALE

A scale where the key signature contains no sharps or flats and where the home note is C, is said to be a *C-major* scale. More specifically, if it includes *open strings*, it is the *Open position C-major* scale. The scale is defined C ⑤ to C ②—plus an upper extension of four notes to G ① and a lower extension of five notes to E ⑥.

As before, set your guitar aside and follow the step-by-step procedure described above, beginning with low C on ⑤ and 2 strokes per note:

Ex. 36

You may also practice the open-position C-major scale alternating between *m* & *i*, *a* & *m*, or *m* & *a*.

1 stroke per note

To prepare for playing one stroke per note, practice the following open string exercise, carefully watching the hand and maintaining a consistently firm stroke in sounding each string:

Ex. 37

Adding the left hand to the above right-hand pattern produces the scale with one stroke per note. Practice slowly at first, gradually increasing the tempo when secure.

Ex. 38

Ex. 39 is a reading exercise. First scan the exercise to determine its general shape and design. Solfege and visualize before playing isolating any challenging movement forms; then practice slowly and accurately. Gradually increase the tempo as you become secure with alternation, string crossing, and tone production.

Ex. 39

THIS PAGE LEFT INTENTIONALLY BLANK

THIS PAGE LEFT INTENTIONALLY BLANK

In Memory

Solo No. 45

ADDITIONAL REPERTOIRE OF THE MASTERS

Etude in E minor

D. Aguado

Andante No. 7

F. Carulli

M.M. ♩ = 60

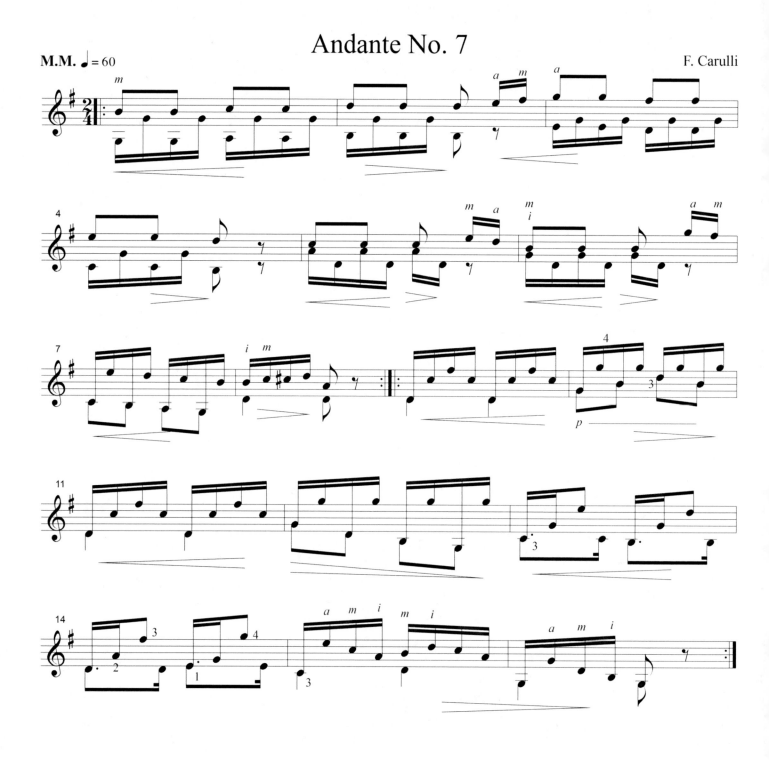

Notice the pick-up measure at the start of the following solo, *Andantino*. Since 2 sixteen notes are the pick-up, count <u>1 e & a, 2 e</u> and begin playing on <u>& a</u>:

Count: 1 e & a 2 e & a

Andantino

Op. 241, No. 19

F. Carulli

Minuetto

M. Giuliani

Fine

D.C. al Fine *

(* no repeats after Da Capo)

Op. 10, No. 1

Allegretto non troppo M.M. ♩= 60

M. Carcassi

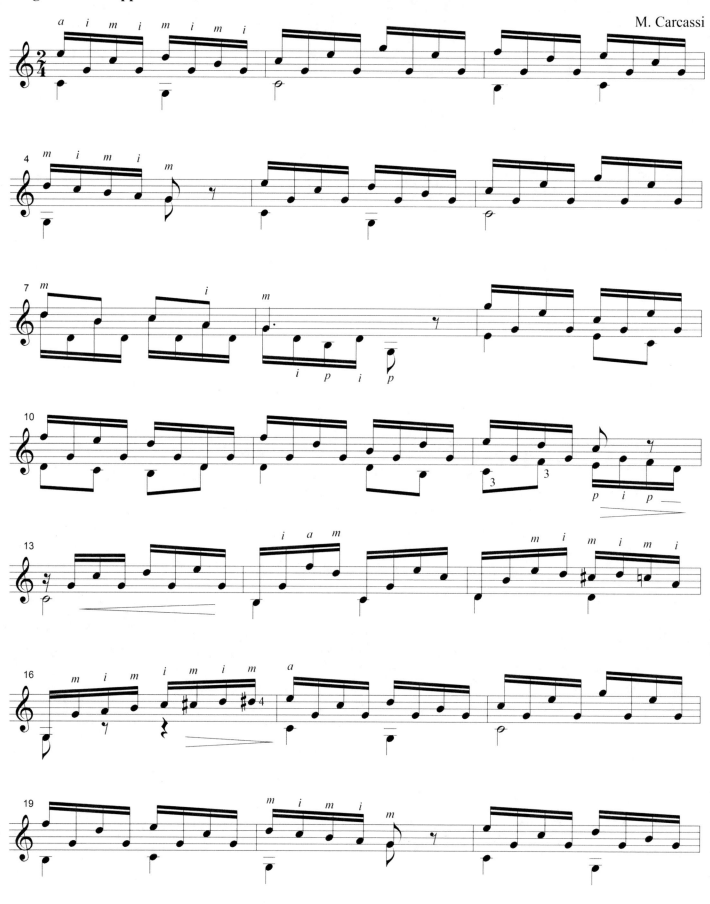

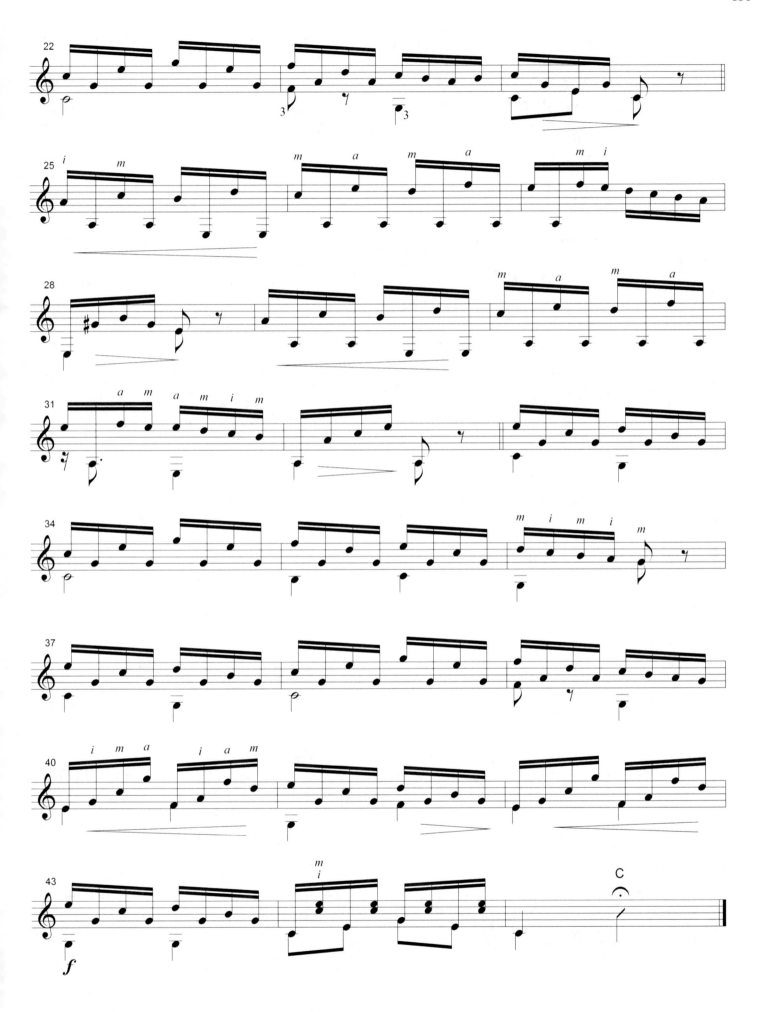

Andante, No. 9

F. Carulli

Glossary of Musical Terms

A tempo	Return to the original tempo.
Accidental	A *sharp* (♯) which raises the pitch by one fret, a *flat* (♭)which lowers the pitch by one fret, or a *natural* (♮) which cancels both sharp or flat.
Coda	Meaning "tail," the ending of a piece which can be an added measure or musical section. A coda may be marked with the sign ⊕
Compound meter	A meter such as $\frac{6}{8}$ where beats can be subdivided into three's.
Crescendo	To gradually play louder, indicated by the sign: ——————◁
D.C. al Coda	*Da Capo al Coda*, meaning to repeat from the beginning of the piece until the ⊕ sign, at which point jump to the coda.
D.C. al Fine	*Da Capo al Fine*, meaning to repeat from the beginning of the piece and stop at the *fine* marking.
D.S. al Fine	*Dal Segno al Fine*, meaning to repeat from the 𝄋 sign and stop at the *fine* marking.
Decrescendo	To gradually play softer, indicated by the sign: ▷——————
Dynamic	The expressive loud or soft indications in music.
Enharmonic	The same pitch but two different note spellings. (e.g., A♭ and G♯)
Fermata — 𝄐	Meaning "to hold" the duration of the note longer. Often found at the end of a piece or musical section.
Forte — f	An expressive marking indicating to play loud.
Indefinite Tie	A tie not connecting to a following note, indicating that the tied note should be held as long as possible.
Key	The musical setting or environment of the piece which provides a sense of arrival and rest as identified by a home note—e.g., the key of C, the key of D, etc.
Key Signature	Shown by accidentals directly to the right of the treble clef, indicating the key of the piece.

Legato	To play in a connected way, occurring when playing with continuity.
Ledger Lines	Extension lines added to the musical staff used for notating notes on strings ⑤ & ⑥.
Meter	The organization (accent pattern) of beats per measure—*triple meter, duple meter.*
Piano—p	To play soft.
Ritard	To slow down.
Simile	To continue expressing in a similar manner.
Simple meter	A meter such as $\frac{2}{4}$ where beats are subdivided into two's.
Solfege	The system of vocalizing notes in the musical alphabet by syllables: *do, re, mi, fa, so, la, ti.*
Staccato	To play in a detached way, occurring when playing with preparation.
Syncopation	To stress weak beats with duration.
Tempo	The speed of the piece.
Time Signature	The two numbers at the beginning of the staff that indicate: how many beats per measure; and what note value is counted as the beat. For example, $\frac{2}{4}$ = $\textbf{2}$ ♩, thus, each measure has the time of two quarter notes.

Index to Compositions

Repertoire from the Master

Additional Repertoire of the Masters

Multimedia Disc Instructions

The multimedia disc contains detailed video lessons for everything in the book. It will play in a standard DVD player or in a computer with a DVD drive.

In addition to video lessons, the multimedia disc contains TNT2 software that you can use to hear professional recordings of various selections in the book. Alter the instrument mixes of the recordings for practice, turn the metronome off and on, loop playback and change tempos for any of the recordings.

For installation, insert the multimedia disc into a computer, double click on My Computer, right click on the CD drive icon, and select Explore. (Mac users can simply double-click the DVD icon that appears on the desktop.) Open the "DVD-Rom Materials" folder, then the "TNT2" folder, and double-click on the installer file. Installation may take up to 15 minutes.

SYSTEM REQUIREMENTS

Windows

7,Vista,XP
1.8 GHz processor or faster
3.4 GB hard drive space, 2GB RAM minimum
DVD drive installation
Speakers or headphones
Internet access required for updates

Macintosh

OS 10.4 and higher (Intel Only)
3.4 GB hard drive space, 2 GB RAM minimum
DVD drive installation
Speakers or headphones
Internet access required for updates

Produced by
Etson Music Corp
3383 F Industrial Blvd.
Bethel Park, PA 15102

Printed and pressed in USA

Distributed by Alfred Music, PO Box 10003, Van Nuys, CA 91410-0003